Content-Area Strategies
Social Studies

WALCH PUBLISHING

GRADES 7–8

1   2   3   4   5   6   7   8   9   10

ISBN 0-8251-6028-6

Copyright © 2002
Updated 2006
J. Weston Walch, Publisher
P. O. Box 658 • Portland, Maine 04104-0658
walch.com

Printed in the United States of America

Table of Contents

Table of Contents *(continued)*

Introduction

The goal of *Content-Area Strategies: Social Studies* is simple: to give students tools
to communicate effectively. This book addresses social studies in terms of a set
of integrated skills and strategies that work together to help students read,
write, speak, and think critically for success in school and beyond. *Content-Area
Strategies: Social Studies* is divided into three instructional sections: Vocabulary,
Reading, and Writing.

Vocabulary

The building blocks of language are words. With this program, students begin
by analyzing words, then synthesize what they have learned to develop
strategies for comprehending new words. The Vocabulary section begins by
introducing vocabulary strategies such as recognizing word parts, looking for
word groups, and looking for context clues. Students then practice the strategies
in a series of activities based on appealing short readings. Building vocabulary
and learning how to figure out new words enhances reading, writing, speaking,
listening, and thinking critically, giving students a broad base of language to
draw on in classroom and real-life communication.

Reading

The second section presents reading strategies. Here, students acquire tools that
help them read to learn. The transition from learning to read to reading to learn
is vital to success in school and in life, and this section helps students broaden
their expectations about text. Familiar patterns of narratives—stories with a
beginning, a middle, and an end—are replaced by organizational constructs
tailored to convey information. In this section, the act of reading is broken down
into a process of steps. Students learn concrete strategies to read informational
texts efficiently, to comprehend what they read, and to retain the information
they have learned. The graphic organizers for the Reading section help students
connect new information to their existing schemata, increasing their ability to
recall and to take ownership of what they read. The reading strategies give
students a way to "see" what they read—a great asset to visual learners.
Organizing and writing what they read also cements information and concepts
in students' minds and helps them retain it.

Introduction *(continued)*

Writing

The Writing section is the third instructional part of *Content-Area Strategies: Social Studies.* In this section, students review the writing process and study models of good writing. Students learn to recognize common social studies informational writing patterns and employ them themselves to write strong essays. The graphic organizers for the Writing section address each explicit step in the writing process. Breaking the process of writing an essay into a series of manageable steps makes the assignment easier to tackle and demystifies the act of writing.

Classroom Management

Content-Area Strategies: Social Studies is easy to use. Each lesson is self-contained and may be used in class or as homework. You may want to model the strategies used in each lesson, showing students that all readers and writers—including teachers—use tools and follow processes to communicate and comprehend. The blank graphic organizers may be photocopied for use in other assignments beyond this book. Students who need more support may benefit from more modeling or from completing some activities and graphic organizers in small groups. Metacognition—talking and writing about learning—can provide structure that supports new information and makes it easier to access. *Content-Area Strategies: Social Studies* transforms the abstract idea of learning into a concrete process that all students can master.

Vocabulary Strategies

Lesson 1
Prefixes and Suffixes

Building Vocabulary

Reading can be a complex process. Whenever you read, you apply decoding skills of various kinds to get meaning from the text. One of those skills—and a vital one—is recognizing and understanding vocabulary.

Vocabulary is the collection of words that you encounter throughout your reading life. In fact, the English language is so rich with words that your vocabulary will probably continue to grow for as long as you continue to read. Increasing your vocabulary will not only make you sound more articulate when you write and speak, it will also increase your understanding of anything else you read and hear.

No matter what you're reading—a textbook, a newspaper article, a popular magazine, a Web page, or the liner notes for some new music—you will understand and appreciate it more if you know what each word means. How can you make this happen?

Strategies to Use

Here are some of the most effective ways to build vocabulary as you read:

- Recognizing word parts like prefixes and suffixes
- Looking for words within words
- Analyzing context clues

Let's first take a look at prefixes and suffixes that can help you decode the word's meaning. Prefixes and suffixes are attached to the central "core" or root of many words of more than one syllable.

Prefixes and Suffixes *(continued)*

Prefixes

Prefixes are word parts that are found at the *beginning* of words. The prefix *pre-* means "before" or "beginning."

Here are some common prefixes to watch for as you read.

Common Prefixes			
ab-	from, off	intra-	within
ad-	to, toward	magn-	large
anti-	against	micro-	small
auto-	self	non-	not
bi-	two	pre-	before
con-	with	pro-	for, in favor of
contra-, counter-	against, opposite	re-	again
		sub-	under, below
dis-	not	super-	above
ex-	out from OR no longer	sym-	together
extra-	beyond	tri-	three
im-	not	un-	not
in-	into OR not	uni-	one
inter-	between, among		

Examples

- *The United States is <u>bisected</u> by the Mississippi River.*

  You know that the prefix *bi-* means "two," so you can make an educated guess that this word means "divided into two sections."

- *One of the goals of Dr. Martin Luther King, Jr. was <u>interracial</u> harmony.*

  You know that the prefix *inter-* means "between" or "among," so you can make an educated guess that this word means "between races."

Prefixes and Suffixes (continued)

Suffixes

Suffixes are word parts that are found at the end of words. Here are some common suffixes you can learn to recognize in your reading.

Common Suffixes			
-able, -ible	able to be	-less	without
-ful	full of	-ly	in such a manner
-hood	condition, state	-ment	state; act
-ion, -tion, -ity	state; quality	-ship	state, condition
-ish	like; having the characteristics of	-some	like, tending to
		-ward	in the direction of
-ive	relating to; having the quality of		

Example

- *The crew of the clipper ship spotted land to the <u>windward</u> side.*

  Since *-ward* is a suffix meaning "in the direction of," you can assume that the crew saw land in the direction from which the wind was blowing.

Prefixes and Suffixes in Action

Read the following passage.

In November 1753, George Washington was asked by the governor of Virginia to investigate the newly built French forts along the Ohio River and to ask the French to withdraw. Washington met with many difficulties along the way, including <u>impassable</u> streams and <u>bothersome</u> weather. When he finally met with the French, Washington commented, "They pretend to have an <u>undoubted</u> right to the river from a discovery made by one La Salle sixty years ago." His <u>counterproductive</u> discussions with the French eventually led to the beginning of the Seven Years War.

The underlined words in the paragraph above may be unfamiliar to you. Your knowledge of prefixes and suffixes can help you decode them. Take the word *impassable*, for instance. It consists of three parts: the prefix *im-* ("not"), the core word *pass* ("to go by or over"), and the suffix *-able* ("able to be"). If you put all three of these meanings together, you get "not able to be passed or crossed over." In other words, Washington found many streams that he could not cross.

Prefixes and Suffixes *(continued)*

The word *bothersome* consists of the core word *bother* ("to worry, trouble, or annoy") and the suffix *-some* ("tending to"). Poor weather tended to bother the travelers in Washington's party.

What about *undoubted*? Take the prefix *un-* ("not") and the familiar word *doubted.* The meaning of this word is "not doubted," or "certain."

Finally, take the word *counterproductive.* The prefix *counter-* means "against" or "the opposite of." The core word *product* means "effect" or "result." The suffix *-ive* means "having the quality of." Taken as a whole, this word means that Washington's discussions with the French were the opposite of having a good effect—they did not have a positive result.

Application

Read the passage below. Then use your knowledge of prefixes and suffixes to answer the questions that follow.

> In 1848 and 1849, the gold rush lured thousands of fortune hunters from all over the world to California. In a number of <u>uninhabited</u> wilderness areas, one canvas city after another sprang up nearly overnight. In places like Sacramento and Stockton, men dug <u>feverishly</u> for the <u>subterranean</u> gold dust that could bring up to five hundred dollars a day for the lucky. However, once the gold was <u>extracted</u> from the earth and sold, many fortunes were foolishly lost through drinking, gambling, horse trading, and other wild behavior. There was a general feeling that the gold supply would last forever. As one prospector wrote of his fellow diggers, "They had found gold at every step and looked on the supply as <u>inexhaustible</u>." Of course, this assumption was proved wrong in the years that followed.

1. The word *uninhabited* means

    (a) not occupied

    (b) not behaving in a socially acceptable way

    (c) crowded

    (d) not having a regular routine

    How were you able to figure out the meaning of this word?

    ____

    ____

Prefixes and Suffixes *(continued)*

2. *Feverishly* means

    (a) at a reasonable pace

    (b) in high temperatures

    (c) with intensity

    (d) with little hope

    How were you able to figure out the meaning of this word?

    ____

    ____

3. *Subterranean* refers to something that is

    (a) under the sea

    (b) under the earth

    (c) in a ship

    (d) hidden in a tunnel

    How were you able to figure out the meaning of this word?

    ____

    ____

4. The word *extracted* means

    (a) blown up

    (b) sold

    (c) moved on tracks

    (d) removed

    How were you able to figure out the meaning of this word?

    ____

    ____

5. *Inexhaustible* describes something that is

    (a) not causing pollution

    (b) never running out

    (c) extremely tired

    (d) not asleep

    How were you able to figure out the meaning of this word?

    ____

    ____

Lesson 2
Word Forms

You have explored using prefixes and suffixes to figure out the meaning of unknown words. Another strategy to use is to look for the "core" of a word to determine its meaning. Once you have found that core—that "word within a word"—decoding the whole word becomes easier.

For example, the word *establishment* contains the core word *establish* (a verb meaning "to set up, to found"). Once you know the basic meaning of *establish,* you can reason that the *-ment* ending turns the core word into a noun meaning "something set up or founded." In fact, you can apply your knowledge of any core word to work out the meanings of all the other forms (or parts of speech) it might take.

Here are some examples of different formations a core word can take.

Adjective	Noun	Verb	Adverb
decisive	decision	decide	decisively
democratic	democracy	democratize	democratically
necessary	necessity	necessitate	necessarily

Notice that certain word endings show which part of speech a word is. Words that end in *-ate* are often verbs. Words that end in *-ity* or *-ness* are usually nouns. Words that end in *-ive* or *-ous* are usually adjectives. And words that end in *-ly* are usually adverbs.

Word Forms in Action

Read the following passage.

The Caribbean is the American Mediterranean in a <u>strategic</u> as well as a <u>climatic</u> sense . . . . The superb arc of islands [the West Indies] has an amazing <u>fertility</u>; the extension of sugar culture around 1650 made even the smallest of them <u>immensely</u> valuable, and the slaves imported from Africa thrived beyond all <u>expectation</u>.

From Morison et al., *The Growth of the American Republic,* p. 48.

The underlined words in the paragraph above may seem difficult. Attacking the words logically makes them much more manageable. For example, the first two words—*strategic* and *climatic*—both end in *-ic,* which is typical of many adjectives. What core words do these two adjectives contain? *Strategy* (meaning "a large-scale plan") is the core word in the first case. *Climate* (meaning "usual or average weather conditions") is the core word in the second. *Strategic,* therefore, means "having to do with strategy," and *climatic* means "having to do with climate."

Word Forms *(continued)*

What word within a word does *fertility* contain? The answer is *fertile* ("rich in resources, fruitful"). The *-ity* ending (which turns adjectives into nouns) gives this word the meaning "the condition or state of being fertile."

How about *immensely?* The word within a word here is the adjective *immense*, which means "enormous, huge." The *-ly* ending usually turns adjectives into adverbs, as is the case here. The meaning of *immensely*, therefore, is "to an enormous extent."

Finally, the word *expectation* contains the core word *expect* (a verb meaning "to look for, to anticipate"). The suffix *-tion,* which turns verbs into nouns, gives this word the meaning "the state of being expected."

Application

Read the passage below, then answer the questions that follow. Remember to look for the "words within words" as you analyze each underlined item.

> Despite this tendency to territorial disputes, Indians did not . . . have "ancient" or "traditional" enemies. Each group surely had its allies and [foes], but such relationships were neither permanent nor necessarily long-lived. Alliances changed . . . both before and after European contact. Probably far more frequently than they fought with each other, different peoples learned from each other. Absorbing new influences . . . did not signal the decay or diminution of any culture.
>
> From Milner et al., *The Oxford History of the American West*, pp. 15–16.

1. The word *tendency* means

    (a) a trend or inclination

    (b) being present, attending

    (c) boredom, tediousness

    (d) connecting tissue between bones

    The core word in *tendency* is ___________________________. (*Hint:* It is a one-syllable verb meaning "to lean, to be directed in a certain way.")

2. The word *territorial* means

    (a) very frightening

    (b) a special breed of dog

    (c) third in a series

    (d) relating to land or property

    The "word within a word" in *territorial* is the noun ___________________________.

    This means ____.

Word Forms *(continued)*

3. The ending of *necessarily* indicates that this word is

    (a) an adverb

    (b) an adjective

    (c) a verb

    (d) a noun

    The core word in *necessarily* is _________________________, which means

    ____.

4. *Alliances* means

    (a) having a certain geographic location

    (b) joining of groups for a common purpose

    (c) deception, lying

    (d) foreigners entering the land

    The two-syllable core word in *alliances* is _________________________, which

    means ____. This word

    form (or part of speech) is a/an _________________________.

5. The word *diminution* means

    (a) very low intelligence

    (b) lessening, fading

    (c) faulty weapon

    (d) two nations joining together

    Diminution is a noun of four syllables; the three-syllable verb form of this

    word is ____.

<u>Lesson 3</u>
Using Context Clues

We have looked at two ways to decode unfamiliar words: recognizing word parts and looking for words within words. Now let's take a look at the third strategy—analyzing context clues.

Analyzing Context Clues

What does the phrase *context clues* mean? Context clues are the parts of a reading that surround a word or phrase you don't know and that can shed some light on its meaning. Some examples of context clues might be

- a definition before or after the unfamiliar word or phrase
- a synonym or an antonym near the unfamiliar word
- examples in the text that illustrate the meaning of the unfamiliar word or phrase
- restatement of the basic meaning of the unfamiliar word or phrase

Context Clues in Action

Read the following passage.

The husband of Loreta Velázquez had always <u>vacillated</u> about which side he should take in the Civil War. He was born in Texas, which was part of the South. Like many other Southerners in the U.S. Army, he was divided between loyalty to the Union, which gave him his career, and his family's <u>allegiance</u> to the Confederate South. He wavered between the two sides. Velázquez, having been raised in the South, convinced her husband to quit his job with the Union army and join the Confederate army. As soon as he went east to begin training for battle, she formed a plan to join him. Since women were <u>prohibited</u>—forbidden by law—to be soldiers, she decided to disguise herself as a man.

Velázquez went to New Orleans in early 1861 to carry out her plan. First, she had a tailor sew a special padded uniform that made her waist appear larger and more masculine. Then she had a barber cut and style her hair to resemble that of a man. Next, a trusted male friend helped her glue on a false mustache. He also helped her practice disguising her voice and feminine <u>mannerisms</u>, like tossing her head and taking short, dainty steps. Finally she selected the name Lieutenant Harry T. Buford, CSA. The transformation was complete.

Adapted from *Latino Heroes of the Civil War* by Michael Walbridge. ©1997 by J. Weston Walch, Publisher.

Using Context Clues *(continued)*

In this passage, some challenging words have been underlined. At first glance, these words may appear baffling. However, you can begin to make sense of them by analyzing context clues. The following is an example of how you might use context clues to figure out the meaning of new words.

The first underlined word, *vacillated*, is not defined or explained in the sentence in which it occurs. But I see that the next two sentences restate *vacillate's* meaning: Velazquez's husband "was divided" between loyalty to the North (the Union) and the South (the Confederates). He "wavered" between the North and the South. Let me try substituting "was divided" or "wavered" for *vacillated*. That works! "The husband of Loreta Velazquez had always been divided about which side he should take in the Civil War." Now I know that *vacillated* means "felt divided" or "wavered between."

The next underlined word is *allegiance*. In the first part of the sentence, I see what looks like a related phrase: "he was divided between loyalty to the Union . . . and his family's allegiance to the Confederate South." The related term for *allegiance* is *loyalty;* I think they are synonyms.

Prohibited, the next underlined word, is actually followed by a definition: forbidden by law.

The fourth underlined word, *mannerisms*, is followed by a couple of examples: "like tossing her head and taking short, dainty steps." These are examples of ways of moving—gestures—that are sometimes considered typically feminine. Maybe *mannerisms* means "typical gestures or habits."

Using Context Clues *(continued)*

Application

Read the following passage. Then use what you have learned about context clues to answer the questions.

Samuel Adams was born in Boston in 1722. His father, also named Samuel, was a wealthy businessman and an important figure at the Old South Meetinghouse and thus was referred to as Deacon Adams. At fourteen, young Samuel Adams entered Harvard, as expected of the son of a Boston <u>dignitary</u>. There are no records of his academic career, but it is probable that at Harvard Adams became familiar with John Locke's powerful written argument *Of Civil Government.* In this <u>treatise</u>, Locke set out his <u>doctrine</u> that every citizen had natural rights of life, liberty, and property. This position also meant that a ruler could not take property from his or her subjects in the form of taxation without their consent.

Adams graduated from Harvard in 1740 and went on to receive his master's degree in 1743. In 1748, Deacon Adams died, and Samuel inherited his father's business, which supplied malt to brewers. Under Samuel's control the business soon began to weaken, then to fail. What really came to interest Samuel Adams was politics. By 1763, he had joined the <u>Caucus</u> Club. This was a secret organization that met in advance of all town meetings to decide upon the slate of candidates for office and what the stands would be on various issues.

Adapted from Critical Thinking Using Primary Sources in U.S. History *by Wendy S. Wilson and Gerald H. Herman. ©2000 by J. Weston Walch, Publisher.*

1. Based on your reading of context clues, how would you define the word *dignitary?*

   ____

   ____

   What examples can you find in the reading to support your definition?

   ____

   ____

Using Context Clues *(continued)*

2. How would you define *treatise*?

    ____

    ____

    What context clue helped you in your definition?

    ____

    ____

3. How would you define *doctrine*?

    ____

    ____

    What context clue helped you in your definition?

    ____

    ____

4. How would you define *caucus*?

    ____

    ____

    What context clues helped you in your definition?

    ____

    ____

Lesson 4
The Shakers and Their Village

Activity 1: Introducing Vocabulary in Context

Read the following article. While you read, notice the words in bold type. Try to figure out what those words mean by looking at the context.

You're at the gate of a Shaker village in the early 1800s. Everything looks orderly and peaceful, but busy. It seems like an ideal place. But this **utopia** is not a dream. During this time, there were many such **settlements** in America. Different groups built towns and villages around a religious or social idea. The Shakers were the most successful and longest lasting of any of these groups.

The Shaker movement began in the mid-1700s in England, as an offshoot of the Quakers. In the 1770s, leader Ann Lee and her followers brought Shakerism to America. They wanted freedom and land so that they could practice their ideas. In the words of a Shaker hymn, " 'Tis the gift to be simple." Upon joining, each member gave up or turned over all his or her worldly **goods.** No personal property would be allowed. Families could join, but the man and woman no longer lived as husband and wife. The feeling of the village was somewhat like a **monastery,** except for the manner of worship. Monks often also farmed and made their own clothes and food, but they prayed quietly in a church. The Shakers' worship included dancing, whirling, and limb-shaking. Like other Christian groups, they took their **doctrine** from select parts of the Bible. But elders, both male and female, had the power to adapt the teachings as they saw fit.

The Shakers wanted to keep their daily focus on God. So everything they used or made to sell was very simple. To help feed, clothe, and house hundreds of people, they created many clever machines and tools. The Shakers did not **patent** these inventions because they did not believe in personal ownership. So anyone in the outside world was free to copy the items and sell them. To this day, many pieces of furniture and other products are sold as "Shaker." The Shakers are now known more for their style than their religion, which does not please them.

Many of the Shakers' other ideas had a widespread effect on American thought. One was **conservation,** or the wise use of resources. Daily activities revolved around it. Another idea was **pacifism.** During all of America's major wars, the Shakers refused to take up arms. During the Civil War, some were **drafted** into the army, but President Lincoln excused them from service. Still they were of much help in feeding and treating the wounded of both sides, difficult as that was. They believed in a practical peace.

At their peak in the early 1800s, the Shakers had 18 villages that housed and employed 6,000 people in several states. Their successful system was **communist,** before that became a negative word. All goods and profits were held in common. Today, at the dawn of the twenty-first century, there is still one Shaker village left with a half-dozen members. The place they made enables them to share their lives as they always did, with "hands to work and hearts to God."

The Shakers and Their Village *(continued)*

Activity 2: Developing Vocabulary in Context

Read each context clue below. Write the word from the box that corresponds to the clue. Then write a new sentence using that vocabulary word.

communist	goods	patent
conservation	monastery	settlements
doctrine	pacifism	utopia
drafted		

1. "refused to take up arms" (explanation clue): ___________________

   ____

2. "wise use of resources" (definition clue): ___________________

   ____

3. "did not believe in personal ownership. . . . So anyone . . . was free to copy the items and sell them" (antonym / experience clue): ___________________

   ____

4. "ideal place" (synonym clue): ___________________

   ____

5. "goods and profits . . . held in common" (description clue): ___________________

   ____

6. "personal property" (synonym clue): ___________________

   ____

7. "towns and villages" (definition / synonym clue): ___________________

   ____

8. "village . . . Monks . . . prayed" (summary clue): ___________________

   ____

9. "into the army . . . service" (explanation clue): ___________________

   ____

10. "teachings" (definition clue): ___________________

    ____

The Shakers and Their Village *(continued)*

Activity 3: Extending Vocabulary Strategies

Read the word origins and definitions below. Write each vocabulary word from the box next to its definition.

communist	goods	patent
conservation	monastery	settlements
doctrine	pacifism	utopia
drafted		

1. from Middle English *settlen*, to seat or bring to rest, + Latin *mentum*, concrete object or result, + s, plural; means "new villages" __________________

2. from Greek *ou*, no, + *topos*, place; means "an imaginary, ideal place"

   ____

3. from Old English *god*, good; means "personal property" __________________

4. from Latin *patere*, to be open (as in open to public inspection); means "to claim an exclusive right" __________________

5. from Latin *doctrina*, teacher/doctor; means "principle within a system of belief"

   ____

6. from Middle English *draght*, to draw, + ed, past tense; means "called to military service" __________________

7. from Greek *monazein*, to live alone; means "a house for persons under religious vows" __________________

8. from Latin *commun*, common, + ist, one who does; means "one who believes in holding goods and profits in common" __________________

9. from Latin *com*, with, + *servare*, to keep, + suffix *tion*; means "careful protection of" __________________

10. from Latin *pax*, peace, + *fic*, doing, tending to, + *ism*, act or practice; means "act of opposing war or violence" __________________

Lesson 5
Henry David Thoreau at Walden Pond

Activity 1: Introducing Vocabulary in Context

Read the following article. While you read, notice the words in bold type. Try to figure out what those words mean by looking at the context.

Henry David Thoreau was born in Concord, Massachusetts, in 1817. In his short lifetime—he died at age 44—he did enough and wrote enough to inspire people all over the world to this day. Thoreau is considered the father of the modern **environmental** movement. He may be best known for his close association with nearby Walden Pond. His study of the weather, the woods, the pond, and living things (humans included) was published in a book called *Walden* in 1854.

In 1845, Thoreau built himself a small house on the shore of Walden Pond for about $28. There he lived for two years, closely observing nature and reflecting on humankind. There was much to study at Walden. It had already been used for over 200 years by white settlers. Indeed, it had a life story, a human and natural **history,** stretching back thousands of years. Thoreau was very good at finding arrowheads. These and other American Indian **artifacts** were everywhere around Walden.

Perhaps at Walden Pond Thoreau found a connection to make up for his being at odds with **society** at large. He didn't behave as most people of his time did. He found it false to conform for the sake of conforming. His first job, as a schoolteacher, ended after two weeks because he refused to beat his students. Moving from teaching to odd jobs, he started spending most of

his time thinking and writing about the subjects that interested him. Those included his dislike of material things and modern inventions, and his hatred of **slavery,** the ownership and forced labor of other human beings. In 1859, he wrote "A Plea for Capt. John Brown." Brown was an **abolitionist,** a person who fought against slavery. Despite Thoreau's plea, Brown was hanged for his violent attack on U.S. government property.

Thoreau's **political** views are as famous as his nature writings. His outspoken opinions on government and laws in the nineteenth century affected such leaders as Mohandas Gandhi and Dr. Martin Luther King, Jr., in the twentieth. His words and ideas have been used countless times by those fighting **tyranny,** or oppression by the government. Thoreau may be best known throughout the world for his 1849 essay **"Civil Disobedience."** In it, he said that if you don't agree with what your government is doing, you should not follow the rules it sets down. Thoreau's refusal to pay his poll tax in protest of the Mexican War landed him in jail for a night. Refusing to pay taxes, refusing to serve in the army, and allowing oneself to be led to jail for protesting are all methods of **passive resistance.** It was this method, inspired partly by Thoreau, that allowed Gandhi to lead India to independence from Great Britain.

Henry David Thoreau at Walden Pond *(continued)*

Activity 2: Developing Vocabulary in Context

Read each sentence below. Choose the word or phrase from the box that matches the meaning of the underlined word or phrase, and write it on the line. For help, refer to the context clues in the story.

abolitionist	history	slavery
artifacts	passive resistance	society
civil disobedience	political	tyranny
environmental		

1. Thoreau found a great <u>story</u> of human and animal habitation at Walden.
    ____

2. Pottery, arrowheads, bones, and shells are all examples of <u>articles</u> found on American Indian sites. _______________________

3. Walden Pond is of <u>ecological</u> interest; it was formed by the melting of the glacier about 10,000 years ago and is not fed by springs or streams, yet it is about 102 feet deep. _______________________

4. Thoreau stepped back from Concord <u>social life</u> but found friendship with other writers, such as Emerson. _______________________

5. Thoreau and his friends spoke and wrote against <u>the abuse of African Americans as unpaid labor</u>. _______________________

6. Thoreau believed that <u>oppressive government</u> should be fought with words, actions, and even nonactions. _______________________

7. Fiery John Brown, admired by Thoreau, was a(n) <u>advocate for the end of slavery</u> who often used violence to make his point. _______________________

8. Thoreau himself once took a more low-key approach to <u>not following laws</u> by refusing to pay his poll tax. _______________________

9. People can fight unfair laws through methods such as <u>refusal to cooperate</u>, for instance, refusing to go to the back of the bus. _______________________

10. Thoreau's views on <u>governmental and legal</u> affairs did not always make him popular. _______________________

Henry David Thoreau at Walden Pond *(continued)*

Activity 3: Extending Vocabulary Strategies

Part I. Cloze Paragraph

Use one of the vocabulary words from the box to fill in each blank in the paragraph.
You may use each word or phrase only once.

abolitionist	environmental	tyranny
civil disobedience	passive resistance	

Henry David Thoreau admired (1)________________ John Brown for fighting
against slavery. He believed that the (2)________________ of the government should
be met with some kind of (3)________________, or refusal to obey laws. Thoreau's
ideas are still used today around the world by people trying to protect both liberty and
natural resources. Some (4)________________ activists have tried to save old-growth
forests by means of (5)________________, such as building a house in an ancient tree
and living in it to keep the tree from being cut down.

Part II. Word Origins

Below are five words from the lesson. Following them are word origins and definitions.
Find the vocabulary word in the box that fits each description below. Write the proper
word in the blank.

artifacts	political	society
history	slavery	

1. from Greek *istor*, knowing or learned; means "tale or record of important events"
    ____

2. from Latin *sclavus*, person of Central Europe held as a servant; means
    "ownership of human beings as forced laborers" ________________

3. from Latin *arte*, by skill, + *factus*, made; means "handmade objects representing a
    culture" ________________

4. from Latin *socius*, companion; means "group of people having common interests"
    ____

5. from Greek *politikos*, citizen, + *al*, relating to; means "having to do with
    government and lawmaking" ________________

Lesson 6
Zora Neale Hurston and the Folklore of the Deep South

Activity 1: Introducing Vocabulary in Context

Read the following article. While you read, notice the words in bold type. Try to figure out what those words mean by looking at the context.

Folklore consists of the original stories, songs, and jokes common to a certain group. It is the subject of serious study by **anthropologists.** These are people, usually college professors, who study human culture. They try to present their findings in a scientific way. In the 1920s, a different kind of anthropologist came along. Her name was Zora Neale Hurston.

Hurston was born in Eatonville, Florida, in 1891. Eatonville was a different kind of town, the first in America set up to be run by African Americans. Its citizens did not face as much **prejudice** as other blacks in the South. White people could not judge and limit them as much. Zora was one of Eatonville's best and brightest. She moved to New York City and studied with a famous anthropologist.

The 1920s and 1930s were the height of Hurston's career as a folklore collector and novelist. This was an exciting time in black history. After World War I, new jobs in the cities of the North attracted thousands of African Americans from the South. This **migration,** or movement of people, is called the Great Migration. In New York, Harlem became the center of an explosion of black culture, including music, theater, and writing. This special era has come to be called the Harlem **Renaissance.** It was a rebirth of interest in African-American origins and arts. In New York, Zora became friends with several famous black writers.

Hurston went back to Eatonville to gather folklore. She shared her own lively personality and absorbed their humor and spirit. Many of the stories in the **rural** Deep South at that time were about, or were handed down from, the **plantations.** These stories from the country reflected a time when whites owned large farms on which blacks worked as slaves. The stories generally told a truth about life in a way listeners could relate to. The **dialect,** or manner of speech (southern black English), was also familiar. These versions of "place" gave the people a sense of roots. In many cases, their own family histories had been lost.

Hurston was doing brave and important work. The growing black middle class in the North, however, did not always like Zora's salty style. Her fiction and folklore seemed to fulfill white **stereotypes** of how blacks lived and talked. These set ideas did not affect Zora. She went on to collect black folklore from other parts of the South and from the Caribbean and to publish books. Later in life Zora was not as successful. Her books were almost forgotten. Writer Alice Walker rediscovered Hurston's work in the 1970s. She found that Zora had died in **poverty** in 1960 and was buried in an unmarked grave. Walker arranged for a stone to be added. It reads: "Zora Neale Hurston, A Genius of the South."

Zora Neale Hurston and the Folklore
of the Deep South *(continued)*

Activity 2: Developing Vocabulary in Context

Read each context clue below. Write the word from the box that corresponds to the clue.
Then write a new sentence using that vocabulary word.

anthropologists	migration	prejudice	rural
dialect	plantations	renaissance	stereotypes
folklore	poverty		

1. "not as successful," "books . . . almost forgotten," "unmarked grave"
    (experience clues): ___________________

    ____

2. "rebirth of interest in . . . arts" (definition/example clue): ___________________

    ____

3. "from the country" (comparison clue): ___________________

    ____

4. "original stories, songs, and jokes common to a certain group"

    (definition clue): ___________________

    ____

5. "movement of people" (definition clue): ___________________

    ____

6. "people, usually college professors, who study human culture"
    (definition clue): ___________________

    ____

7. "white," "set ideas" (comparison/explanation clue): ___________________

    ____

8. "farms on which blacks worked as slaves" (definition clue): ___________________

    ____

9. "manner of speech" (definition clue): ___________________

    ____

10. "White people could not judge and limit them"
    (explanation/antonym clue): ___________________

    ____

Zora Neale Hurston and the Folklore
of the Deep South *(continued)*

Activity 3: Extending Vocabulary Strategies

Fill in the following chart with the vocabulary words from the box. You may use each word only once.

anthropologists	migration	prejudice	rural
dialect	plantations	renaissance	stereotypes
folklore	poverty		

Zora's job:

worked as _________________

to collect _________________

New York City, 1920s–1930s:

the Great _________________

fueled the Harlem _________________

Zora Neale Hurston's World

Historical black problems:

racial _________________

white _________________

struggle up from _________________

Folklore collected:

concerning _________________

in _________________ South

spoken and written in _________________ form

Research Skills

Find and read some of Zora Neale Hurston's folktales. You might try reading her book *Of Mules and Men.*

Lesson 7
César Chávez and Migrant Workers in California

Activity 1: Introducing Vocabulary in Context

Read the following article. While you read, notice the words in bold type. Try to figure out what those words mean by looking at the context.

In the early 1960s, conditions were bad for California's thousands of **migrant** workers. These workers travel from farm to farm to pick crops as they ripen. They usually live in tents, cabins, or trailers. In the early days, their children did not receive much education. The camps were not clean. The migrants worked long hours for low pay. But many of the workers were in the United States illegally. They didn't complain too loudly, for fear of losing their jobs.

Migrant workers are used in many states. In California's Central Valley, they are very important. The Central Valley is a 450-mile-long center of **agribusiness.** It produces a great deal of America's food. Cheap **labor** helps make the farms profitable.

Migrant workers have always been underpaid. By the 1960s, **wages** had increased to only 90 cents an hour for most workers. And there were no **benefits**—no overtime pay, no healthcare or savings plans, no education, not even clean drinking water or decent restrooms in the fields.

In 1965, someone came along who wanted to make a difference. César Chávez was the son of migrants and was raised in the camps. He left school in the sixth grade and later served in the U.S. Navy during World War II. From 1952 to 1962, he worked for a community service group in California. Then Chávez and another person from that agency, Dolores Huerta, began the first field workers' **union.** Both **activists** felt that having the workers present their complaints as a group would help bring change.

The union began talking with the growers, trying to get improvements. Those were slow in coming—too slow. Chávez and the union decided some real action was in order. In 1965, they began a **strike** to get better wages for wine-grape pickers in California. This work stoppage continued, with little reaction from growers. In 1966, Chávez led a 340-mile march to call attention to the problems of migrant workers. And then in 1968, Chávez and the union called for a nationwide **boycott** of table grapes. If fewer people bought grapes, the growers would lose money. And if the growers lost money, maybe they would begin to listen. Schools, churches, and other groups joined in. By 1970, the boycott was working. Many growers signed union agreements promising improvements.

Some call Chávez and Huerta **radicals.** They undertook actions that people might call extreme. But they asked whether it was extreme to ask for decent working conditions or a living wage. Chávez and the union continued to work for the laborers through the 1970s and 1980s, even as union membership sometimes sank. Chávez's death in 1993 brought about renewed interest in the union, now called the UFW, or United Farm Workers. His efforts for workers' rights live on.

César Chávez and Migrant Workers in California *(continued)*

Activity 2: Developing Vocabulary in Context

Each vocabulary word in the box fits one of the descriptions below. Refer to context clues in the story to figure out which word fits each description. You may use each vocabulary word only once.

activists	labor	strike
agribusiness	migrant	union
benefits	radicals	wages
boycott		

1. work: _____________________

2. one who moves from place to place for work: _____________________

3. large employer for farmwork: _____________________

4. payment for work: _____________________

5. extra payment for work: _____________________

6. organized group of workers: _____________________

7. refusal to work: _____________________

8. refusal to buy the products of someone's work: _____________________

9. people who plan activities, possibly to help workers: _____________________

10. people who sometimes perform extreme actions in working for a cause:

   ____

Dictionary Skills

Agribusiness is what is known as a *portmanteau* word. A portmanteau is a type of travel bag. In a portmanteau word, two or more words are folded up together into one. From what two words is *agribusiness* formed? The word *brunch* is also a portmanteau word. From what two words is it formed? Can you think of any other portmanteau words? Look them up in a dictionary.

César Chávez and Migrant Workers in California *(continued)*

Activity 3: Extending Vocabulary Strategies

Each vocabulary word in this lesson comes from one or more roots. The meaning of each root is given in the right-hand column. Try to fill in the left-hand column with the matching vocabulary words by using the root meaning.

activists	labor	strike
agribusiness	migrant	union
benefits	radicals	wages
boycott		

Vocabulary Word   **Meaning of Root**

1. _____________________   work

2. _____________________   oneness, togetherness

3. _____________________   drive or do + one who does

4. _____________________   rootlike, growing from the base

5. _____________________   to go

6. _____________________   name of English person who was shunned

7. _____________________   one who moves or changes

8. _____________________   pledges, promises

9. _____________________   favor, promotion

10. _____________________   farm + (financial) activity

Lesson 8
Commuters and the Suburbs

Activity 1: Introducing Vocabulary in Context

Read the following article. While you read, notice the words in bold type. Try to figure out what those words mean by looking at the context.

In the late 1800s, a change began in America. As cities became more crowded and dirty, wealthy families with summer homes outside cities began living there full-time. Businesspeople got into the city by streetcar or train. Beginning in the 1920s, when cars began to become popular, the general movement increased. After World War II, returning soldiers and their new families moved outside the cities by the thousands. Now the American **suburbs** were no longer a **trend;** they were a way of life. A single-family house on a private lot became "the American dream." The **baby boom** increased the number of people who would live that dream. Between 1946 and 1964, 76 million Americans were born.

America's postwar wealth kept growing. The rich got richer. They stayed in their expensive city neighborhoods or at their country estates. **Racism** and other problems kept the poor in the inner cities or in the countryside. America was called a "melting pot" of races, but many people still did not have a fair shot at the American dream because of their skin color or country of origin. But the **middle class,** which was mostly white, demanded and got a new standard of living. The government did everything it could to help create that lifestyle. It offered low-interest loans on houses. It built wide roads and the new interstate highway system. That made **commuting** to jobs in the city easier. Businesses helped, too. They offered credit plans that let people make purchases over time.

The **affluence,** or wealth, that caused the growth of the suburbs in the 1950s and 1960s changed the fabric of American life. Once people had lived within walking distance of shops, jobs, and schools. Now daily life centered on the use of the car. Front porches, where people used to gather, shrank to sets of steps that were never used, unless they were near the driveway. Watching TV and shopping at malls became the common forms of entertainment.

As the suburbs grew, businesses moved to them. Unfortunately, people still did not always live and work in the same town. So traffic increased, from morning and evening rush hour to all day long. Older suburbs began to seem too much like the cities they surrounded. A new trend developed: the **exurbs**—the suburbs beyond the suburbs. In the 1980s and 1990s, baby boomers built bigger and bigger homes on bigger and bigger pieces of land. "Big box" stores went up between the suburbs and the exurbs. This **sprawl,** or uncontrolled development, began to eat up open space.

No one really knows where suburban sprawl is going to end. It may be that people will begin to move back to where it all began: the village or the small town. Recently, a new element has also appeared on the scene: the **telecommuter.** This is a person who has given up his or her job in the city and works from home using new technology. It remains to be seen what effects these new commuters will have on society and the suburbs.

Commuters and the Suburbs *(continued)*

Activity 2: Developing Vocabulary in Context

Complete each sentence below with a vocabulary word from the article. Then write the context clue or clues from the article that showed you the meaning of the word. You may use each vocabulary word only once.

affluence	commuting	middle class	sprawl	telecommuter
baby boom	exurbs	racism	suburbs	trend

1. Beginning in the late 1800s, moving to the suburbs was a(n) _______________.

   Context clue(s): ____

2. America's _______________ after World War II meant that many families could afford to buy a house and a car.

   Context clue(s): ____

3. The American _______________ was neither rich nor poor and in the postwar era was mostly white.

   Context clue(s): ____

4. In the 1950s and 1960s, thousands of middle-class people moved to the _______________ outside the major cities.

   Context clue(s): ____

5. _______________ between home and work by car or train enabled workers to have the best of both worlds, city and suburb.

   Context clue(s): ____

6. During the _______________, millions of new Americans were born.

   Context clue(s): ____

7. _______________ throughout the 1960s kept many Americans from rising up out of poverty and pursuing the American dream.

   Context clue(s): ____

8. In the 1980s and 1990s, people began to move even farther from the cities, to the newer _______________.

   Context clue(s): ____

9. Urban and suburban _______________ began to eat up farmland and other open space between developed areas.

   Context clue(s): ____

10. This century may become the age of the _______________, who can work from any location and live wherever he or she pleases.

    Context clue(s): ____

Commuters and the Suburbs *(continued)*

Activity 3: Extending Vocabulary Strategies

Fill in the chart below with vocabulary words from the box. You may use each word only once. When you have filled in all the blanks, unscramble the letters that are boxed to complete the mystery phrase.

affluence	commuting	middle class	sprawl	telecommuter
baby boom	exurbs	racism	suburbs	trend

AMERICAN SUBURBIA

Causes and Indicators

There was a(n) __ __ __ __☐ toward moving out of cities.

Postwar ☐__ __ __ __ __☐__ __ gave people money to move.

The __ __ __ __ __ __ __   __ __☐__ __ was a rapidly growing social group.

A(n) __ __ __ __ __   __ __ __☐ produced many children, for which parents needed more space.

White Americans' ☐__ __☐__ __ also influenced flight from cities.

Two Ways to "Go"

Do __ __☐__ __ __ __ __ __ between home and city.

Become a __☐__ __☐__ __ __ __ __ __ __ and work at home.

Effects

Thousands of homes were built in __ __ __ __☐__ __ on edges of cities.

Then __ __ __☐__ __ became an unattractive feature of the landscape.

The aging of suburbs leads to the building of new ☐__ __ __ __ __ and more sprawl.

Mystery Phrase

Chasing the __ __ __ __ __ __ __ __ __   __ __ __ __ __ __

Glossary

abolitionist: a person who undertakes measures to do away with slavery

activists: people who undertake vigorous action to achieve a goal

affluence: wealth, abundance

agribusiness: the production, storage, and distribution of food and farming supplies

anthropologists: people who study human beings and their cultures

artifacts: products of human activity, usually handmade

baby boom: population surge caused by an increase in births

benefits: payments or services provided as part of a work contract

boycott: refusal to buy or use a product or service in order to get provider's attention

cabinet: a body of advisers to the president

civil disobedience: refusal to obey laws and rules, usually for a specific reason

communist: holding goods and enterprises in common rather than privately

commuting: traveling between home and job or school regularly

conservation: careful protection of something, such as a natural resource

dialect: a regional version of language

doctrine: a principle or order to follow within a system of belief

drafted: called to military service

environmental: having to do with the condition of natural surroundings

exurbs: regions beyond the suburbs, usually occupied by the well-to-do

folklore: customs, stories, songs, and jokes common to a certain group of people

goods: worldly possessions; items that could be sold or bartered

history: a story or record of important events

labor: work, usually manual, or the group of people who do that work

middle class: a social group that is neither rich nor poor

migrant: a person who moves regularly to find work

migration: the movement of people from one place to another

monastery: a house or community for people who have taken religious vows

pacifism: the act of opposing war or violence

passive resistance: the refusal to cooperate with government by means such as sit-ins

patent: to claim the sole right to do or make something

plantations: large farms, worked in the pre-Civil War South by slave laborers

political: having to do with government and/or the making of laws

poverty: the state of being poor or in want

prejudice: preformed set of negative ideas about a person or people

racism: prejudgment or discrimination based on skin color or national origin

radicals: people who take extreme actions to get attention for important social issues

renaissance: a rebirth of interest in something, particularly in the arts

rural: having to do with the country rather than the city or the town

Glossary *(continued)*

settlements: new towns or villages

slavery: the holding and treatment of human beings as property and forced laborers

society: a community, nation, or group of people having common interests and activities

sprawl: irregular or uncontrolled real estate development

stereotypes: fixed mental pictures, or opinions, about a group or groups of people

strike: work stoppage undertaken in protest of wages or conditions

suburbs: residential areas outside a city, but within commuting distance

telecommuter: a person who works from home using telecommunications devices, such as e-mail, telephones, videoconferencing, and fax machines

trend: a growing movement or tendency

tyranny: oppressive power over citizens

union: a group of workers organized for the common purpose of bargaining with employers

utopia: an imaginary, ideal community or place

wages: payments for labor or service

Reading Strategies

Lesson 1
Previewing

When you sit down to read an e-mail from a friend or a magazine article about a sports star, you probably don't go through any complicated procedure. You just read it, enjoy it, then go on your way. When you need to read in order to gather and retain information (for school, let's say), the reading process requires a little more work.

The Reading Process

Good reading actually involves these three stages:

1. Prereading (before reading)

2. Reading

3. Postreading (after reading)

In the lessons that follow, we will take a closer look at each of these stages of reading and what they can mean to you. Let's start with prereading.

Prereading Steps

Prereading (just as the *pre-* prefix implies) is what you do before you read. Prereading involves four steps. These steps are sometimes called the "4 Ps."

Prereading

1. Preview

2. Predict

3. Prior knowledge

4. Purpose

You can organize these steps in a 4-P chart like the one below. Eventually, you will not need a chart. For now, you can use the 4-P chart to remember and practice the prereading steps.

4-P Chart

1. Preview	2. Predict	3. Prior Knowledge	4. Purpose

Previewing *(continued)*

The Importance of Previewing

When you go to the movies, you probably arrive in time to see the previews of coming attractions. What are these previews for? They are designed to spark your interest in new movies. A preview tells you what an upcoming movie is about—the main characters, key events in the plot, and perhaps a problem that needs solving.

In the same way, a first look or preview of something you are about to read can give you important clues about what that reading contains. Previewing helps you get the most important information from your reading, and it helps you remember that information longer.

Previewing

To preview a new chapter in your history book or a long article in a news magazine, what do you do first?

1. **Start with the title.** The title usually tells you the main idea of the entire chapter or article.

2. **Scan** the chapter or article, looking for any highlighted text that is meant to stand out. Watch for headings and subheadings. Be alert for boldfaced or italicized words within paragraphs. Pay attention to bulleted or numbered lists and what they seem to be about.

3. **Look at the graphics** in your reading selection. Graphics are photos, drawings, maps, charts, graphs, time lines—any text elements that are not just words.

4. **Skim** the chapter or article. When you skim, you do not read word for word. You should read the first and last paragraphs in each major section of the text. If you are working with a shorter passage, read the first and last lines in each paragraph.

Previewing *(continued)*

Application

Use your prereading skills to preview the following selection from a United States history text. Do *not* read the entire article—just preview it! Fill in the Preview column of the 4-P chart that follows the article.

The Nation Keeps Growing (1793–1874)

Time Line

Events Elsewhere	Date	Events in America
	1793	Whitney invented cotton gin
	1803	Louisiana Purchase
	1807	Fulton used steam to power *Clermont*
	1812–14	War of 1812
Napoleon defeated at Waterloo	1815	
	1818	National Road
Mexico gained freedom from Spain	1821	
	1822	Austin guided Americans into Texas
	1825	Erie Canal completed
	1828	Andrew Jackson elected president
	1830	Cooper developed steam locomotive
Slavery abolished in Britain	1833	
	1836	Texas free from Mexico; Battle of Alamo; Whitman's mission in Oregon
	1840	McKay's clipper ship
	1844	Morse developed telegraph
	1845	Howe invented sewing machine; Texas became a state
	1846	Mexican War began; U.S. acquired Oregon Country
	1848	End of Mexican War; gold discovered in California
	1849	California gold rush
	1850	California became a state
	1853	Gadsden Purchase
	1860	Pony Express began

Previewing *(continued)*

Territorial Expansion

At the dawn of the nineteenth century, the United States had grown from thirteen colonies into a nation that was beginning to claim international recognition. After the Louisiana Purchase, effected by President Thomas Jefferson, the nation's western border now extended far beyond the Mississippi River, and its northern and western borders now included a major portion of the Missouri River. The country had doubled its territory in a relatively brief time.

Achievements in Transportation and Communication

In order for a nation to remain united and effective, there must be an easy and efficient way for people, goods, and ideas to move from one part of the country to another. Five important technological developments helped bring most parts of the new nation closer together by speeding transportation and improving communication. These involved roads, canals, steamships, railroads, and telegraph lines.

Early **roads** were narrow, potholed, and muddy when it rained. Therefore, just before the beginning of the War of 1812, the government started building the **National Road.** When it was finally finished, it ran from western Maryland to central Illinois—the finest road in America at the time. People traveling on this road bought supplies in the towns and villages located along the way. Many merchants benefited from this business, and the resulting prosperity helped many of the towns to grow.

For transportation by water, a major innovation was the building of **canals.** Canals were dug to connect bodies of water where no natural waterways existed. Horses or mules walking on land pulled canal boats or barges through the water. Such travel was cheap but slow. The governor of New York, De Witt Clinton, soon realized how valuable this cheap transportation could be. He arranged for the building of the **Erie Canal,** which connected the New York cities of Albany and Buffalo. When the 363-mile-long canal was finished in 1825, it was possible to go by boat from New York City to the Great Lakes in about ten days.

Until 1807, the only way to move a boat upriver or against the current was by using oars, poles, or towropes powered by men or mules. Eventually, an American named Robert Fulton decided that a steam engine could be used to power a ship. Many people thought that Fulton was wrong; his first **steamship,** the *Clermont,* was called "Fulton's Folly" by skeptics. Then, one day in 1807, the *Clermont*'s huge paddle wheel began to turn, driving the ship up the Hudson River. On that historic voyage, Fulton's ship traveled 300 miles in just over 60 hours. The age of steam transportation had begun.

Adapted from *Short Lessons in U.S. History,* by E. Richard Churchill and Linda R. Churchill. © 1999 by J. Weston Walch, Publisher.

Previewing *(continued)*

Ask yourself these questions to help you fill in the Preview column of the 4-P chart. Some information has been filled in to get you started.

1. What does the chapter title tell you about the main idea of this reading selection?

2. What concepts are expressed in the headings and subheadings?

3. What key words are highlighted in the text?

4. When you skimmed the first and last paragraphs, and the first and last sentences in each paragraph, what ideas seemed to be most important?

5. What graphic elements are included? What do these graphics emphasize?

4-P Chart

1. Preview	2. Predict	3. Prior Knowledge	4. Purpose
1. Territorial expansion			
2.			
3. Key words: roads—National Road canals—Erie Canal			
4. Key ideas: U.S. doubled territory— 19th century Importance of easy transport and communication			
5.			

Lesson 2
Predicting

Have you ever seen television commercials or magazine ads promoting the services of people who claim to be able to "see" the future? These services may promise to tell you what will happen later in your life. These people are claiming to predict what will happen to you at some future date.

Prediction may not work very well in fortune-telling, but it is a powerful tool in reading. In order to get the maximum benefit from what you read, you should make predicting a regular strategy in your reading process.

Application

Using the information you gathered during the previewing stage (see Lesson 1), you can now predict what you think will happen in the reading on page 38. Here are some key questions to help you predict what the reading is all about. Use these questions to help you fill in the Predict column of the 4-P chart.

1. Based on your preview, what do you think this reading passage focuses on?

2. Which topic (or topics) seems to be covered in the most depth in this reading?

3. What do you think you will learn from your reading?

4. What do you think the main idea or thesis of this reading might be?

4-P Chart

1. Preview	2. Predict	3. Prior Knowledge	4. Purpose
	1. focuses on transportation development 2. 3. will tell what developments were . . . 4.		

Lesson 3
Prior Knowledge

What happens when you begin to read something new? Do you just read the words and let them flow into your mind? Is your brain like an empty container, which this new reading material will simply fill up?

The answer is "no." Reading is never a completely passive activity. Whenever you read, you bring your own life experience to the reading. In many cases, you will already know something about the subject covered in the reading selection. This information you already possess is called your **prior knowledge.**

When you read, you make connections between the information in the text and the prior knowledge in your head. Successful readers are active readers, always drawing from their storehouse of prior knowledge, relating it to what they're reading, and adding any new information to that store.

Application

You have already previewed the reading on page 38, and you have made some predictions about it. Now, make some connections between what you think the reading is about and what you already know about this subject—your prior knowledge.

Now do some brainstorming. Look back at the 4-P columns you have filled in for Lessons 1 and 2. What words or ideas come to mind when you think about this topic or these topics? Write as many related words, facts, and thoughts as possible in the Prior Knowledge column below.

4-P Chart

1. Preview	2. Predict	3. Prior Knowledge	4. Purpose

Lesson 4
Purpose

The Reader's Purpose

Why do people read? There are many reasons. Some people love reading for its own sake. They read for enjoyment.

Others read to gather information. They read a daily newspaper, perhaps subscribe to a weekly newsmagazine, and may on occasion tackle a nonfiction book—a political biography, for example. They are reading to be well informed.

Still others read only when it is required—by a classroom teacher, or by a supervisor on the job to develop special workplace skills. These people choose to devote time to reading only when there is a clear educational purpose or specific reward (perhaps better grades or higher pay). They read to learn.

Application

Before you start to read, ask yourself what your purpose is. Your answer will help you determine which reading strategies to use. For the article you've been working with on page 38, your purpose has been mainly to practice the prereading steps. Imagine now that you have been assigned the article for social studies class. In the 4-P chart below, fill in what your purpose for reading would be—what do you want to gain by reading?

4-P Chart

1. Preview	2. Predict	3. Prior Knowledge	4. Purpose

42

Purpose *(continued)*

The Writer's Purpose

Why do people write? Again, there are many reasons. Some authors write for the sheer enjoyment of it. They write out of love for the craft, out of a desire to tell good stories and give pleasure to others. They write primarily to entertain.

Others write to let the public know about the world around them. They may become news writers, art critics, or authors of history and biography. They write to inform. Other writers want to share some special knowledge with a very particular audience. They write how-to books, algebra texts, or medical papers. They are writing to teach.

Author Bias

In an earlier lesson, you learned that readers bring their personal experience, or prior knowledge, to a piece of reading. In the same way, every author brings his or her own personal experience to a piece of writing. This influences what the author chooses to write about and how he or she writes it. In fact, authors can sometimes feel so strongly about a subject that their emotions or judgments color their writing. They may leave out facts that contradict their personal opinions, or they may include information that is not necessarily proved to be true. Writing that is slanted toward one viewpoint at the expense of another is biased writing. It is important to consider the writer's viewpoint, or author bias, every time you read.

Now read the entire passage on page 38. When you have finished, answer the following questions.

1. Did your prereading activities prepare you for what you actually learned when you read the whole passage? Why or why not?

    ____

    ____

    ____

2. What was the author's purpose in writing the passage? Why do you think so?

    ____

    ____

    ____

Lesson 5
Introduction to Reading Strategies

Now that you have learned and practiced the four key prereading steps, you can turn your attention to the second stage in the overall reading process: the reading itself. How do you get the maximum benefit from the reading stage?

Graphic Organizers

One way successful readers learn and retain information is by using graphic organizers. Despite the fancy name, graphic organizers are really just simple charts that you can make and use yourself. While reading, you fill in your graphic organizer. It helps you arrange your thoughts, note key concepts and terms from the reading, and clarify the main ideas.

Since writing something helps to reinforce it, the act of filling in a graphic organizer makes new material easier for your brain to recall. In addition, the visual arrangement of the words and concepts in a graphic organizer gives your brain a "picture" of the information you need to remember.

Kinds of Graphic Organizers

Here are some of the most effective graphic organizers used by readers.

KWL—The KWL organizer consists of three sections: (1) **K** = what I already **know** about a particular subject; (2) **W** = what I **want** to know about the subject; and (3) **L** = what I **learned** about the subject from the reading.

SQ3R—This organizer consists of five sections, each representing a step in the reading process: (1) **S** = survey; (2) **Q** = question; (3) the first **R** = read; (4) the second **R** = recall; (5) the third **R** = reflect.

Semantic Web—This type of graphic organizer can take many different forms. It usually consists of a central circle (or other shape) representing a main idea or main character in the reading. Supporting ideas and details then branch out from the center, forming a more or less complex web.

Outline—Outlining is the most linear of the graphic organizers. An outline helps the reader arrange material in a methodical, step-by-step manner. Outlines often reflect the skeleton of a reading selection.

Structured Notes—This type of organizer can take a variety of forms. The goal is to help readers arrange their notes in a systematic, logical manner based on the structure of the reading selection.

Lesson 6
KWL

As you learned in Lesson 5, the letters in KWL stand for

K = what I already know (about the topic)

W = what I want to know (about the topic)

L = what I learned from the reading

The K and W steps involve the prereading process. **K** asks for the reader's prior knowledge (what I already know), and **W** seeks a purpose for reading (what I want to learn). This is the sort of information you would find in a 4-P chart. The **L** step is what happens after reading (the postreading process), when the reader asks, "What did I learn from this?"

A typical KWL organizer looks like the one below.

K	W	L
Prior **know**ledge—some facts about this topic that I have already learned; concepts I already **know**	What else I **want** to know about this topic; questions I have that give me a purpose for reading	What I **learned** from this reading; new facts, ideas, or viewpoints that I had not considered before

KWL in Action

The following passage is about French Renaissance castles. The KWL chart that follows it has been filled in for you. Study the **K** and **W** sections of the organizer first; then read the passage. Finally, look at the **L** section of the organizer to see what the reader learned. Is there anything you might add?

KWL *(continued)*

During the French Renaissance, the royalty and noble families of France were greatly influenced by the impressive artistic achievements of their Italian neighbors. Hoping to capture some of the style and elegance of artists like Da Vinci and Michelangelo, the French aristocracy either built magnificent new chateaux (castles) or added major additions and ornaments to their existing medieval homes.

The most splendid chateaux—including Chambord, Chenonceaux, Azay-le-Rideau, and Usse (the inspiration for the Sleeping Beauty legend) — were built between the mid-1400s and the late 1500s. Scores of such chateaux are still to be found (and visited) in the Loire River valley, southwest of Paris. This is where the kings of France hunted, entertained, plotted, and ruled during most of the Renaissance. These days of glory ended when Henri IV moved his court back to Paris at the close of the sixteenth century.

K What I KNOW	W What I WANT to Know	L What I LEARNED
Renaissance = came after the Middle Ages France's capital is Paris. Castles = where wealthy and powerful lived; offered protection from enemies	When did this happen? Where were these castles built? Do they still exist?	mid 1400s–end of 1500s Loire valley = SW of Paris Many exist; can be visited. One chateau inspired Sleeping Beauty story. This (not Paris) was where kings actually ruled for many years.

Application

Look at following passage about the Ming Dynasty. What do you already know about the subject? Jot down what you know in the space under the **K** in the graphic organizer that follows the reading. In the space under the **W,** write what else you want to know about this subject. Now read the passage.

KWL *(continued)*

The last native Chinese dynasty in history was the Ming, succeeding the Mongols and ruling a vast empire from 1368 to 1644. Ming rule began under a rebel leader named Zhu. The dynasty's first emperor, he was given the name Hongwu. As supreme head of state with absolute power, Hongwu ordered the killing of thousands of government officials and provincial leaders who resisted his rise to power. He created a strong central government, which at first unified the huge and diverse empire.

Most citizens lived and worked on small farms throughout the Chinese countryside, receiving little or no education, while the educated elite—including a large class of civil servants—lived in large cities like Nanjing (the new capital), Beijing, and Guangzhou. The population, now better fed than in earlier centuries, grew from 60 million at the dawn of this dynasty to about 150 million at its close.

The Ming had an enormous impact on Chinese art and culture. They were best known for their beautiful porcelains and ceramics (which were often exported), works of literature, and silk and cotton weaving. The Ming dynasty also sponsored many daring sea explorations, built the Great Wall, laid out new roads, and constructed the Great Canal linking Beijing with the Yangtze and Huang He rivers.

Eventually, Ming authority in the capital began to weaken as Mongol invaders on the northern border, Japanese pirates on the south coast, and overtaxed peasants within the empire itself made repeated attacks that the centralized government could not defend itself against. Defeated by a foreign tribe in Manchuria in 1619, Ming rule began to unravel. The northern invaders made further encroachments into Chinese territory until they founded the Qing dynasty, which officially began in 1644.

What did you learn from this reading? Write your answers in the space under the **L** in the KWL chart below.

K **What I KNOW**	W **What I WANT to Know**	L **What I LEARNED**

KWL *(continued)*

Quiz

Complete the following statements, which are based on the reading about the Ming dynasty.

1. The word *encroachment* in the last sentence of the passage means

    (a) crouching down, lying low to the ground

    (b) an invasion of harmful insects

    (c) villages or towns surrounded by tall fencing

    (d) trespassing or intruding

2. The Ming dynasty was well known for

    (a) fine regional cuisine

    (b) porcelain and ceramic exports

    (c) daring temple architecture

    (d) a strong educational system for all citizens

3. The population probably received better nutrition during the Ming dynasty because

    (a) there were fewer people to share the food supply

    (b) mothers attended school to learn how to prepare healthier meals

    (c) climate changes lengthened the growing season

    (d) imported items and better transportation gave people more access to good food

4. The Ming dynasty failed largely because of

    (a) foreign invasions and rebellions from the large class of civil servants

    (b) pirate invasions and the fall of the Great Wall

    (c) foreign invasions in the north and the south, as well as peasant rebellions

    (d) lack of money due to too many exports and foreign wars

5. The strong central government of the Ming dynasty

    (a) also proved to be its downfall in the long run

    (b) empowered the peasant classes through its system of irrigation canals

    (c) provided the best military defense against foreign invaders

    (d) served as a model for future governments, including that of the United States

Lesson 7
SQ3R

In an earlier lesson, you learned that another powerful graphic organizer to use when you read is called SQ3R. Although the three Rs in this organizer have meant different things to different people over the years, an effective definition in use today is

S = Survey; Q = Question; R = Read; R = Recall; R = Reflect

Like the KWL organizer, the SQ3R includes some of the prereading steps that you would follow to complete a 4-P chart. For example, the **S** (survey) and **Q** (question) steps fall into the prereading category. SQ3R also involves reading (covered in the first **R**) and postreading (covered in the second and third **Rs**).

Here is what a typical SQ3R organizer looks like.

S	Q	R	R	R
Preview the reading; **survey** text and art. Note key items.	Make predictions. Ask **questions.** Decide your purpose for reading.	**Read** the selection with care; make notes as you read.	Take time to review the reading; on paper, **recall** the most important points.	Think about what you've learned; **reflect** on what this means.

SQ3R in Action

The following reading passage is about economic inflation. The SQ3R chart that follows the passage has been filled in to show you how someone might use this chart while reading. Study the **S** and **Q** sections of the organizer first. Then read the passage. Next, look at the first **R** section to see what was noted during reading. Finally, look at the last two **R** sections to see what the reader learned. Is there anything you might add?

SQ3R *(continued)*

One of the greatest threats to a market economy is **inflation.** Simply put, inflation results in the diminished purchasing power of money. This in turn leads to higher prices. Naturally, higher prices mean that many people can no longer afford to buy the items they want or need. Workers therefore have two choices: to seek higher rates of pay from their employers, or to lower their own **standard of living.** Otherwise, they must borrow money or deplete their personal savings to maintain their current levels of spending.

Most workers first opt to demand higher wages in order to keep up with the inflation rate. As a result of granting pay increases, however, employers then raise the prices of their goods and services. Other consumers have to pay more for the higher-priced items, which means that they in turn need to seek higher pay to maintain their current standard of living. This continuing cycle of increasing prices and wages is called an **inflationary spiral.**

Adapted from *Understanding Our Economy,* by E. Richard Churchill and Linda R. Churchill. © 1998 by J. Weston Walch, Publisher.

S **Survey**	Q **Question**	R **Read**	R **Recall**	R **Reflect**
<u>Key terms</u>: *inflation, standard of living, inflationary spiral* Inflation = threat to economy	What is inflation? <u>Prior knowledge</u>: *standard of living* = way we usually live, spend money	Inflation = less buying power Results in workers seeking more $$ Leads to higher prices (cycle/spiral)	Review definitions of 3 boldfaced terms. Summarize all main points.	People with low or fixed incomes could be at larger disadvantage during inflation—can't raise their pay. Risk of more citizens getting into debt.

Application

The following passage is about the treatment of Japanese Americans during World War II. Using the SQ3R graphic organizer that follows the passage, first survey the reading. Make notes of the most important terms and concepts in the section under the **S.** Then connect these with your prior knowledge and question what else you want to know. Note this in the **Q** section of the chart. Finally, read the passage, jotting down new information in the section under the first **R.**

SQ3R *(continued)*

Two months after a Japanese air bombardment devastated the United States naval fleet at Pearl Harbor, President Franklin Roosevelt signed Executive Order 9066. Dated February 19, 1942, this law ordered the removal of all Americans of Japanese ancestry from their homes. In all, more than 110,000 Japanese Americans—most of whom lived in Hawaii or on the West Coast—were affected.

Virtually none of these citizens was considered a threat to national security by U.S. intelligence agencies. Nevertheless, political leaders from both major parties were swayed by anti-Japanese prejudice on the part of the public. Most members of Congress therefore supported the president's action.

Japanese-American citizens of all ages were rounded up by American military personnel and taken to any one of sixteen temporary "assembly centers," which had been quickly erected in isolated spots, like fairgrounds and racetracks, far from the Pacific coast. Of the sixteen camps, thirteen were in California; the other three were in Washington, Oregon, and Arizona. Most "detainees" were forced to stay in these assembly centers for four or five months, while more permanent—and more isolated—internment camps were built. Eventually, ten such camps were built, most of them in lonely desert areas with harsh climates. There many of the prisoners remained—fed and housed, but deprived of most of the rights supposedly granted to all U.S. citizens—for the duration of the war. In the words of one detainee, "I could never figure out what they thought we were going to do. Born and raised in a typical American home. Middle-income people. Then to have this happen, you wonder why. What'd I do?"

What did you learn from this reading? Try to recall the main points. Write them in the section under the second **R**. Next, take some time to reflect. What does this reading mean to you? What important points is this author trying to make? Note this in the section under the third **R**.

S	Q	R	R	R
Survey	Question	Read	Recall	Reflect

SQ3R *(continued)*

Quiz

Complete the following statements, which are based on the reading about the internment of Japanese Americans.

1. The word *devastated* in the first sentence means

   (a) covered a very large area

   (b) devalued, lowered the price of

   (c) completely destroyed

   (d) changed it from a state to another form of government

2. In the context of the third paragraph, the word *internment* means

   (a) confinement or imprisonment

   (b) training in a medical setting like a hospital

   (c) a place for an apprentice to learn a new skill or job

   (d) a place for reflective thinking and meditation

3. Executive Order 9066 ordered the removal of

   (a) all people visiting the United States from Japan

   (b) all Japanese Americans living on the West Coast

   (c) all Japanese citizens with American ancestry

   (d) all Americans with Japanese ancestry

4. Political leaders probably allowed themselves to be swayed by anti-Japanese feelings because they

   (a) had access to special information about Japanese-American terrorists

   (b) were worried that harm would come to American citizens from the West Coast

   (c) did not want to displease the people who elected them

   (d) wanted to prevent Japanese Americans from moving to Washington, DC

5. Residents of the internment camps were deprived of many rights of citizenship

   (a) including liberty, since they were not free to come and go as they pleased

   (b) including access to shelter and food

   (c) because they had voluntarily given up these rights to prove their loyalty

   (d) because they posed a serious threat to American security

Lesson 8
Semantic Web

Semantic webs can take many different forms. These graphic organizers generally resemble a spider's web. They contain a central circle (or other shape) representing a major idea or a major character in a reading selection. Supporting ideas and details fan or branch out from the central shape, forming the rest of the web. Completing a semantic web can help you sort out main ideas versus details. It can also help you clarify a cause versus its effects.

A typical semantic web might look something like this.

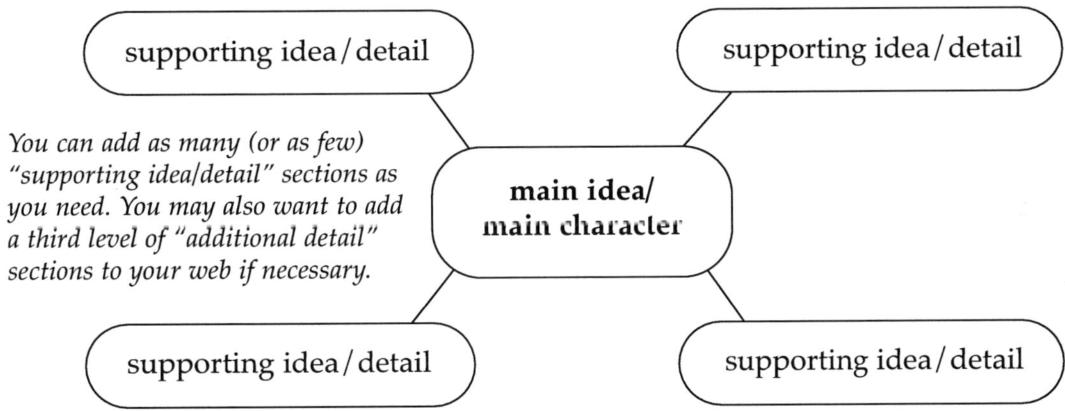

Semantic Web in Action

The reading passage that follows is about an archeological site in Mexico. The semantic web that follows it has been filled in to show you how someone might use this organizer while reading. Read the passage. Then study the semantic web. Is there anything you might change?

Semantic Web *(continued)*

For centuries, the ancient Mexican ruins of Palenque were forgotten deep in the Yucatán, smothered by dense rain forests. An occasional explorer had glimpsed and recorded some of Palenque's marvels, but the reports went largely unnoticed. Those who did pay any heed to this Maya civilization noted a resemblance to ancient Egyptian culture. Some pyramids, statues, and relief carvings found at Palenque did resemble their Egyptian counterparts. Eighteenth-century historians therefore surmised that, at some much earlier point, there had been a colony of Egyptians in Mesoamerica.

Then, in 1840, explorers Stephens and Catherwood made the hazardous trip through the jungle to Palenque. This time, the team took greater care in examining the vine-covered ruins. They discovered a 300-foot-long, stucco-decorated palace complex with a system of courtyards and detailed, grotesque carvings of human figures. They also discovered temples built upon large pyramids, stone tablets carved with unique hieroglyphic writing, and many other remains of a large, sophisticated ancient city. The explorers were convinced that, despite a slight resemblance to Egyptian art, Palenque bore no real traces of Egyptian culture whatsoever: "It is the spectacle of a people . . . originating and growing up here, without models or masters, having a distinct, separate, indigenous existence . . . like the plants and fruits of the soil. . . ." This began a new perception of the Maya as a culture in their own right.

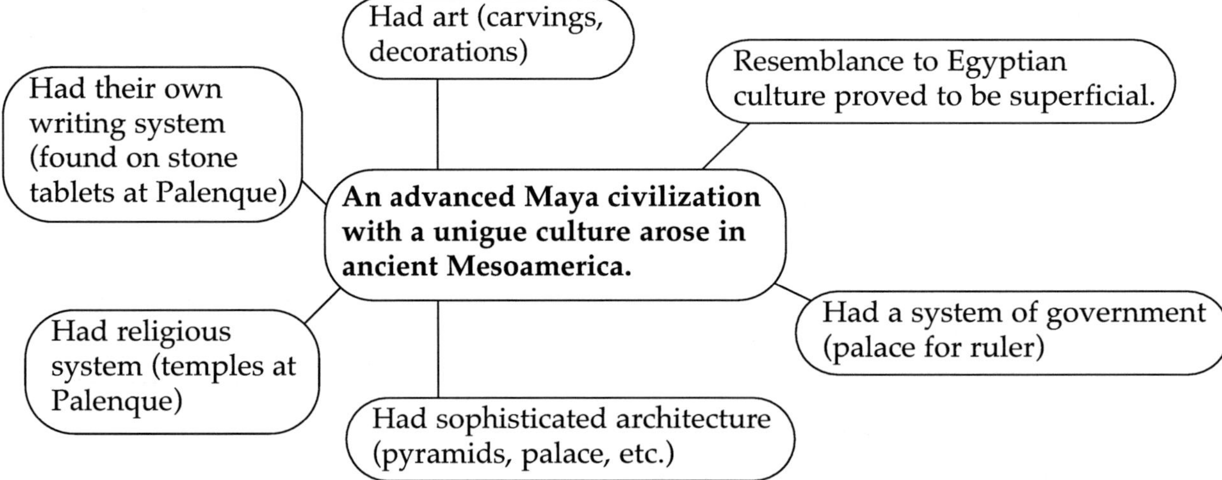

Application

The following passage is about African Americans during the Civil War. Read the selection carefully. Then fill in the semantic web at the bottom of the page to help you record the main idea and details in the reading.

Semantic Web *(continued)*

The Fugitive Slave Act required anyone who captured an escaped slave to return the unfortunate man, woman, or child to the South. During the Civil War, however, Union generals arranged to keep runaways as "contraband of war." This meant that they were enemy property and did not need to be returned. All in all, about 200,000 escaped slaves became paid laborers for the Union cause during the war. They dug trenches, built forts, and loaded supply wagons.

As the war dragged on, many of these laborers became volunteer soldiers, although the U.S. government did not recognize them officially until July 1862. Then Congress passed a law allowing African Americans to be paid for fighting for the Union army. Just a few months later, a black regiment from Kansas was engaged in a battle in Missouri—the first time African Americans had officially fought on American soil.

During the course of the war, many black regiments fought heroically for the North. In July 1863, for example, the Fifty-fourth Massachusetts Regiment took the lead in a major attack on Fort Wagner in South Carolina. Forty-two percent of the regiment were killed or wounded in this one battle; their heroism inspired many other African Americans to enlist.

By the end of the war, black soldiers had undoubtedly helped the Union win the Civil War. The numbers are impressive: 186,000 African Americans served in the Union army; about 29,000 served in the navy. Of these men, a total of 38,000 died in the war. African Americans fought in at least 39 major battles and 400 smaller engagements, from Bull Run to Appomattox. In addition, countless others participated behind the lines, serving as spies, scouts, nurses, and teachers. The contribution of African Americans to the Union's victory cannot be underestimated.

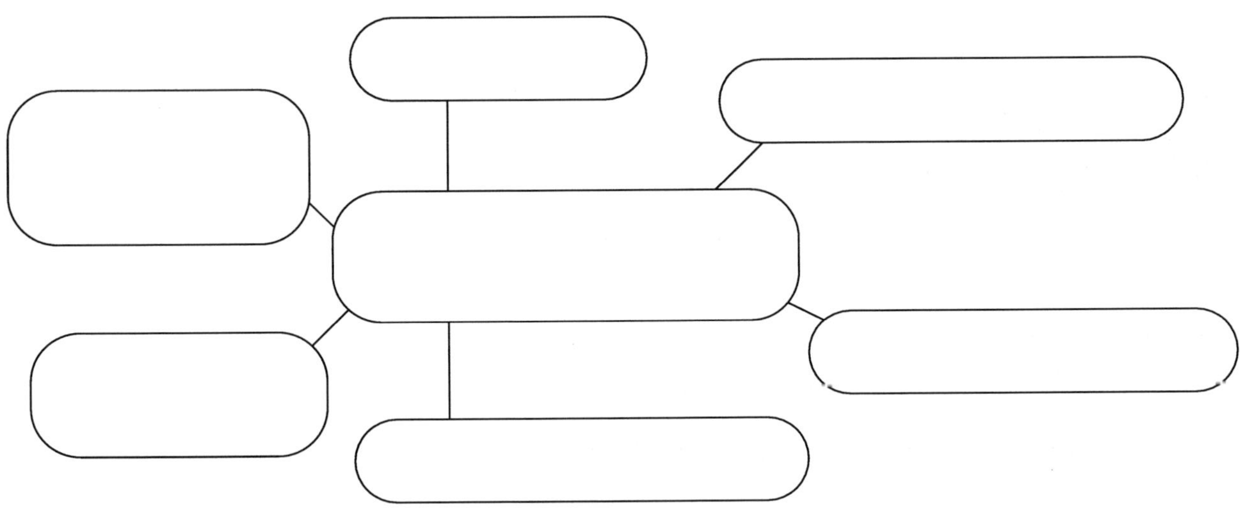

Semantic Web *(continued)*

Quiz

Complete the following statements, which are based on the reading about African Americans during the Civil War.

1. The word *fugitive* means

    (a) useless or futile

    (b) running away

    (c) forgetful, neglectful

    (d) taking refuge

2. A *regiment* is a

    (a) military unit of soldiers

    (b) political system

    (c) regulated system of diet and exercise

    (d) particular geographic location

3. The Union army was interested in keeping escaped slaves as "contraband" mostly because

    (a) they were eager for the reward money from the South

    (b) they needed the labor that the escaped slaves could provide

    (c) it was too difficult to return them to their rightful owners during the war

    (d) the Union generals were staging a formal protest of the Fugitive Slave Act

4. Including black soldiers in the Union army and Union navy, the total number of African Americans who served officially during the Civil War was

    (a) 38,000

    (b) 86,000

    (c) 186,000

    (d) 215,000

5. Many African Americans were actually willing to serve as unpaid volunteers in the early years of the war; this was probably because

    (a) they did not need the money

    (b) the Fugitive Slave Act allowed them to do so

    (c) they had been well trained for battle before enlisting

    (d) they hoped it would help them escape slavery

Lesson 9
Outline

An outline is one of the most step by step, or sequential, of graphic organizers. An outline helps readers—and writers—arrange material in a methodical manner.

Making an Outline

Traditionally, the main ideas are labeled with Roman numerals. Major supporting information is labeled with capital letters. The next level of information is labeled with Arabic numerals, and the level below that, with lowercase letters. A typical outline might look something like this.

Major Subject or Topic (This could be the title of the reading.)

I. Main idea

    A. Detail

        1. supporting information (if applicable)

        2. next supporting information (if applicable)

           a. more information about 2

    B. Second detail

    C. Third detail (if applicable)

II. Next main idea

    A. Detail

    B. Second detail

    C. Third detail (if applicable)

III. Next main idea (if applicable)

Outline in Action

The following reading passage is about the Articles of Confederation. The outline that follows the reading has been completed to show you how someone might use this organizer while reading. Read the passage yourself; then study the outline. Is there anything you might change?

Outline *(continued)*

The Articles of Confederation were voted into life by Congress in March 1781 while the Revolutionary War still raged. The change in government outlined in the Articles simply formalized what had been taking place since 1775, when war first broke out. The Congress of the new Confederation, like the earlier Continental Congress, consisted of members representing each of the thirteen states in the new nation. Each state was allotted between two and seven members, and each member was limited to three years in office out of any six. Each state got one vote.

Some changes in governmental structure included a requirement that nine out of thirteen states (in other words, a clear majority) agree by vote whenever a major congressional decision had to be made. Such possibilities included going to war, raising armed forces, making treaties with other nations, or taking on debt. A final possibility was appointing a new commander-in-chief, or president.

Another change included giving Congress the power to appoint five special governmental departments: foreign affairs, war, the admiralty, finance, and the post office.

Articles of Confederation

   I. Similarities to previous government

      A. members represented all 13 states

      B. each state got 2–7 members

         1. 3-year terms every 6 years

      C. 1 vote per state

  II. Differences from previous government

      A. 9 out of 13 states had to agree by vote for key items

         1. war

         2. raising army

         3. treaties

         4. debt

         5. choosing president

      B. Congress got 5 new departments

         1. foreign affairs

         2. war

         3. admiralty

         4. finance

         5. post office

Outline *(continued)*

Application

The following passage is about the Hawaiian Islands. Read the selection carefully. Then fill in the outline that follows the selection to help you record the main points of the reading. You will probably want to change the outline by adding or removing lines.

The Hawaiian Islands were first settled well over a millennium ago by Polynesians from other islands in the South Pacific. After this original ancient settlement, there were no further known foreign visitors to the Hawaiian island group until the arrival of Captain James Cook in 1778. Thus, for many centuries a unique Hawaiian culture developed from its Polynesian roots, free from any outside influences.

This tropical island chain was formed through a series of volcanic eruptions that occurred hundreds of thousands of years ago. Volcanoes under the ocean floor sent molten lava upward through the water. The lava broke the water's surface, then settled and cooled, forming the beautiful islands that we know today.

Spanning an area that covers more than one thousand miles, the Hawaiian Islands remain geographically isolated. The Aleutians far to the north, and the Marquesas Islands far to the south, are their nearest neighbors—yet both island chains are at least two thousand miles away.

I. ____

    A. ____

        1. ____

        2. ____

        3. ____

    B. ____

        1. ____

        2. ____

        3. ____

II. ____

    A. ____

    B. ____

    C. ____

Outline *(continued)*

Quiz

Complete the following statements, which are based on the reading about the Hawaiian Islands.

1. The word *millennium* means

    (a) one hundred years

    (b) one thousand years

    (c) one million years

    (d) before recorded history

2. The word *molten* in this passage means

    (a) tunneling through the water

    (b) shedding some of its mass as it moves

    (c) melted due to heat

    (d) similar to mold

3. The original settlers of the Hawaiian islands came from

    (a) the Aleutians

    (b) the Marquesas

    (c) Captain James Cook's expedition

    (d) Polynesian islands in the South Pacific

4. The Hawaiian Islands were undisturbed by foreign settlers for many years because

    (a) the Polynesians kept them out

    (b) the volcanoes were too threatening

    (c) they are too rocky for easy landing by ship

    (d) they are physically very distant

5. The Hawaiian culture probably

    (a) retained some Polynesian features

    (b) became very English after Cook's arrival

    (c) was highly influenced by the people of the Aleutians

    (d) was highly influenced by the people of the Marquesas

Lesson 10
Structured Notes

You may have already learned something about taking notes. This may have involved jotting down important facts while researching a term paper. Maybe you wrote down key terms and ideas during a class discussion. However, most of us take notes in a casual way without organizing our thoughts or arranging our notes. Structured notes help readers do just that.

In structured notetaking, your paper is divided into important categories and transformed into a graphic organizer. A structured note page might look like one of the following:

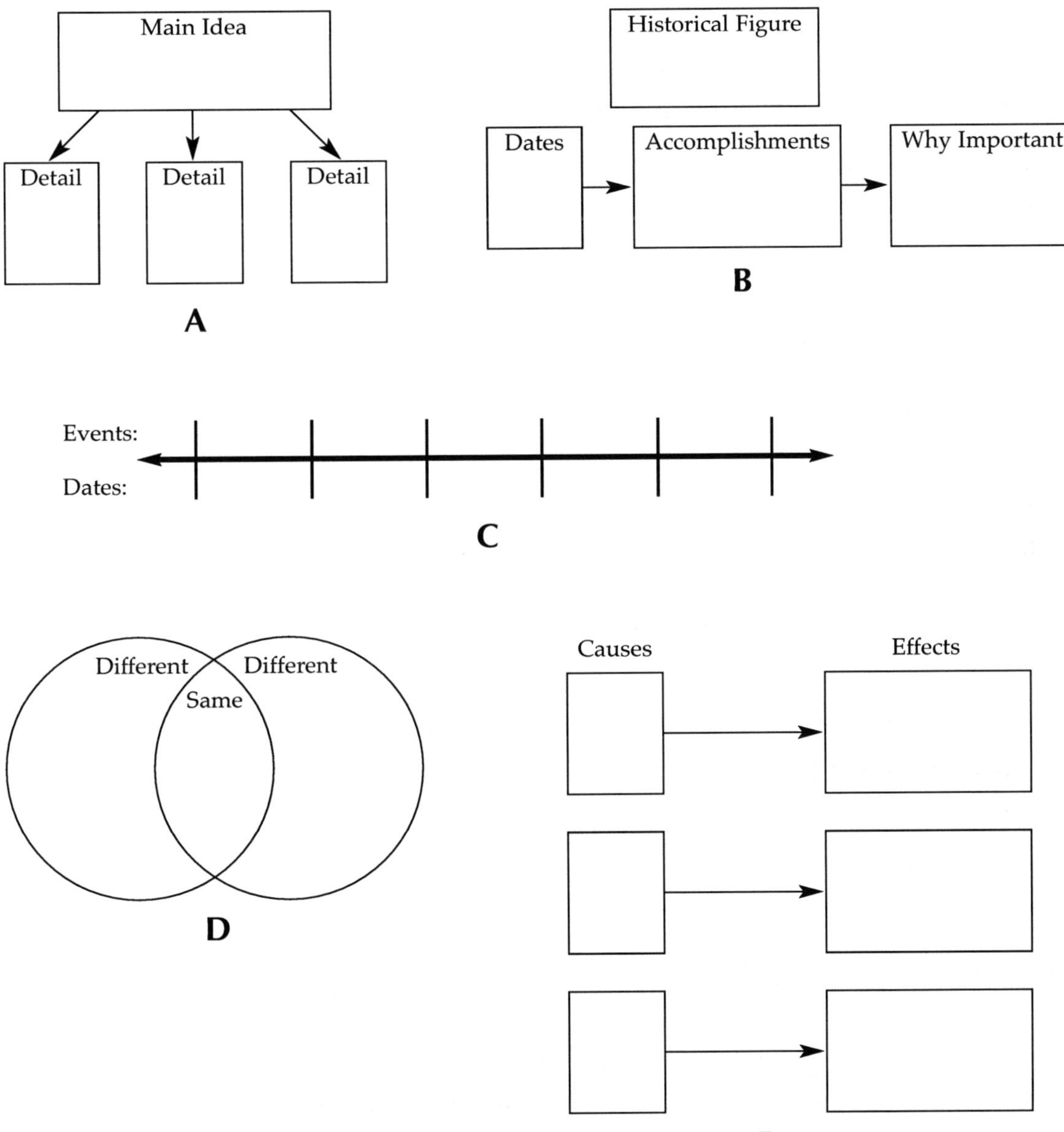

Structured Notes *(continued)*

The exact wording for the headings on your paper will vary according to your reading purpose and the nature of the reading selection itself. If you follow the prereading steps outlined in Lessons 1–4, you will probably have a good idea about which headings will work best.

Structured Notes in Action

Read the passage below. Then look at the structured notes that follow to see how one reader kept track of the material.

In the early 600s, at the time when Muhammad first began preaching, Arabia was largely populated by nomadic tribal peoples known as Bedouins. These wandering groups traveled with herds of sheep and goats over the Arabian peninsula, seeking grazing lands among the many areas of desert. The rest of the Arabian population was concentrated in towns and settlements along the Red Sea or in the southern valleys. The most notable of these settlements were in the Hejaz region in the northwest, Mecca, Medina, and Yemen.

There was no centralized government to speak of in Arabia at this time. Tribal laws and loyalties ruled the lives of most people. The family unit was extremely close-knit and proud, and the Arab's life was largely occupied with family obligations and certain religious observances.

Although Muhammad would soon transform their religious life, Arabs of this era still practiced Zoroastrianism, which emphasized the individual's free will to choose between good and evil in life. All Arabs, regardless of tribe, reserved three months each year to devote to religious ceremonies. During that period, they ceased all fighting and concentrated on prayer and pilgrimage to the Kaaba sanctuary in Mecca, the center of their holy world.

Main Idea	Details
Arabian population in early 600s	➤ Nomadic tribes (Bedouins) —raised sheep, goats A few towns/settlements (Red Sea & valleys in south) —Mecca, Medina, Yemen, Hejaz
Government	➤ Tribal law; no centralized govt.
Social organization	➤ Family unit most important
Religion	➤ Zoroastrianism (good vs. evil) 3 mos./yr. for prayer & peace —pilgrimage to Kaaba (Mecca)

Structured Notes *(continued)*

Application

The following passage is about the early Puritans. Read the selection carefully. Then use the organizer that follows. You may want to change headings or create a completely different graphic organizer. Do what works best for you.

The Puritans who first colonized New England were in fact a small splinter group who had broken away from the powerful Church of England. They were frustrated by the many levels of church officials who dominated their parish priests. They were also deeply disturbed by the extravagance and questionable morals of English society. This small band of farmers, shopkeepers, and manual laborers therefore moved to Leyden, in the Netherlands, in 1609. There they stayed for ten years, worshipping at their own English Congregational Church and living in poverty but in peace.

Around 1619, however, war was threatening in the Netherlands. The Puritans, seeking a different home where they could have complete freedom of religion, decided to try a new life on a very distant shore:

America. A group of generous English merchants agreed to fund their voyage, even obtaining a land grant for the Puritans from the Virginia Company.

In the fall of 1620, in the harshest sailing season of the year, this brave and ill-prepared group set sail in the *Mayflower.* They arrived in Cape Cod Bay on November 11, outside the limits of the Virginia Company's lands. Not knowing where their final settlement would be, but aware of their need to work together to survive, these English citizens quickly wrote and signed an agreement stating that the will of the majority would rule them until further notice. This was the Mayflower Compact, which would prove to be a cornerstone of American democracy.

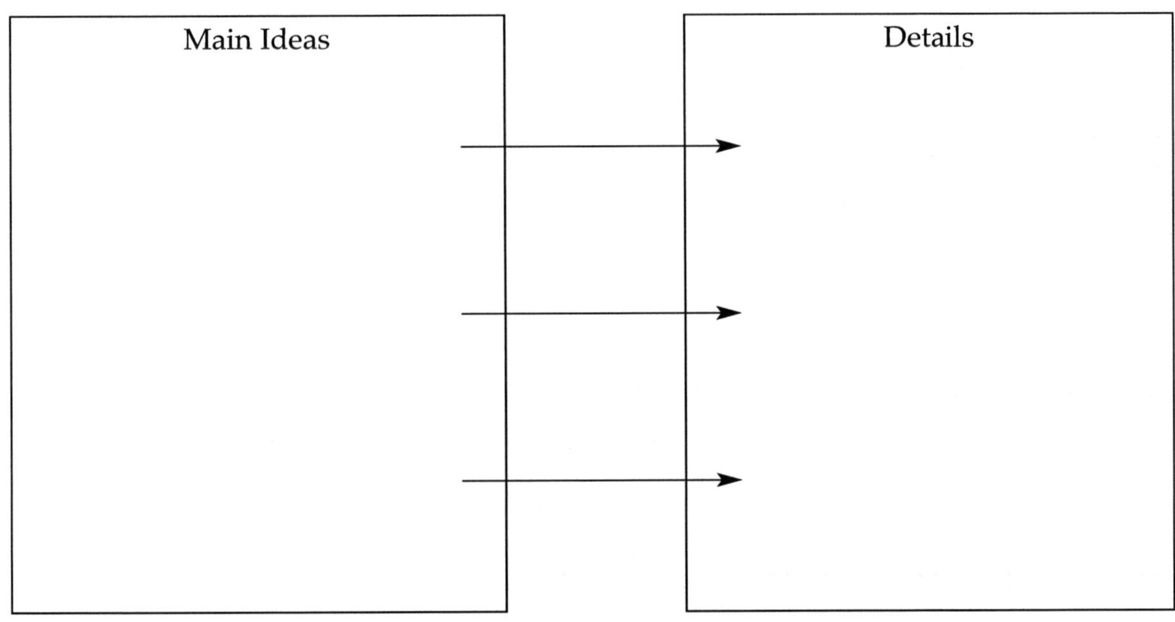

Structured Notes *(continued)*

Quiz

Complete each of the following statements, which are based on the reading on the
previous page about the Puritans.

1. The word *extravagance* means

    (a) going beyond reasonable limits in buying or behavior

    (b) wandering outside, with no home of one's own

    (c) taking things away from others

    (d) getting revenge for a wrong that has been committed

2. To live in *poverty* is to live

    (a) with very little money

    (b) with a great deal of political power

    (c) in small apartment houses

    (d) where the gunpowder for weapons was stored

3. The Puritans chose America for their new home because

    (a) many of them had relatives there

    (b) many New England businesses were offering jobs

    (c) their church in the Netherlands was destroyed in the war

    (d) they wanted to practice their own religion without interference

4. The Puritans were mostly

    (a) of royal or aristocratic birth

    (b) parish priests

    (c) shopkeepers and laborers

    (d) sailors and soldiers

5. The Mayflower Compact was important for two reasons:

    (a) It was written on the *Mayflower,* and it formed a democracy.

    (b) It was written by the Puritans, and it was written in English.

    (c) It was the first Compact ever written, and it formed the Puritans'
         government.

    (d) It gave the Puritans a form of government, and it helped form
         American democracy.

Lesson 11
Summarizing and Paraphrasing

After Reading

What do you do after you finish reading? Do you slam your textbook shut and say, "Finally! That's done—now I can check my e-mail"? Or do you practice postreading strategies? It is important to think about what you have learned from your reading. (Think of the L in the KWL chart.) To do this, you need to spend a little time reflecting on what the text is really saying and what conclusions you can draw from it. (Think of the last R in SQ3R.)

One of the most powerful ways to show that you have really understood a reading selection is to retell it briefly yourself. There are two ways to retell the main points of a reading:

- Summarizing—using words that all come directly from the reading

- Paraphrasing—using mostly your own words

Summarizing and Paraphrasing in Action

The reading passage below is about how companies sell stock. It is followed by a summary and a paraphrase that retell the most important points of the reading passage. Read the passage first. Then read the summary and paraphrase. Do they include all the main points?

When a for-profit business needs funding to expand or to otherwise improve its facilities and products, how does it raise the funds? Many companies choose to sell stock, or shares in the business. By selling stock to a number of people, who then become shareholders, the company can receive the capital it needs in order to grow. At this point, the company offering the stock to outside buyers is no longer a private business. It becomes a publicly traded company, which shares all financial risks—as well as the profits—with its shareholders.

There are three types of shares (or securities) that companies often offer to their investors: bonds, preferred stock, and common stock. Each of these securities offers a different level of financial risk, should the company not perform as well as expected, and a different level of potential reward, should the business succeed.

Summarizing and Paraphrasing *(continued)*

Summary

When a business needs funding, it may choose to sell stock, or shares in the business. The stock buyers become shareholders. Then the business becomes a publicly traded company. It shares the financial risks and profits with the shareholders. There are three types of shares (securities): bonds, preferred stock, and common stock. Each offers a different financial risk and a different level of reward.

Paraphrase

If a company needs to raise money, it may decide to sell stock. Then people who are not employees of the company own a part of the business. When this happens, the business is not private any more; it is a public corporation. All of the stock owners then have a "piece of the pie," so if the business does well, they make money, too; if the business does poorly, so do they. You can get three kinds of shares: bonds, preferred stock, and common stock. They don't cost the same amount of money to buy, and they don't earn the same amount of profit.

Application

The following passage is about Midwestern prairie farmers in the 1800s. Read the selection carefully, using whichever graphic organizer you like to note important information.

In the middle of the nineteenth century, prairie farmers in the American Midwest were the most common kind of pioneer. The fertile land of this region produced bumper crops on a fairly predictable basis, and the rising prices that could be asked for wheat in eastern markets like New York made farming more and more attractive. Moreover, with the arrival of an efficient railway network between 1850 and 1860, prairie farmers could sell their grain and livestock to distant customers without the burden of long, difficult wagon rides.

There were also many innovations in farm technology during this era that made the farmer's life easier and more profitable. Two new kinds of reaping machines (developed by Hussey and McCormick, respectively) sped up the harvest and did the work of many laborers—who were always in very short supply. The harvester (which gathered grain into bundles), the self-knotting binder (which tied the bundles up), the steel plow, and other inventions all transformed prairie farming into a financially solid enterprise.

Now, on another sheet of paper, use the information in your graphic organizer to write a brief summary or a brief paraphrase of the reading. Be sure to indicate which one you are writing.

Summarizing and Paraphrasing *(continued)*

Quiz

Complete each of the following statements, which are based on the reading about prairie farmers in the mid-nineteenth century.

1. The word *innovations* means
    (a) building new inns or hotels
    (b) newly developed things
    (c) clapping hands in an audience
    (d) producing eggs

2. The word *enterprise* in this passage means
    (a) winning a reward or prize
    (b) entering a contest
    (c) a business or project
    (d) something of great value

3. Between 1850 and 1860, farming became more profitable because
    (a) there were so many laborers to help do the farming
    (b) the Civil War kept up the demand for wheat
    (c) many farmers moved back to New York
    (d) a good railroad network was built in the Midwest

4. Eastern markets like New York probably paid high prices for Midwestern wheat because
    (a) the wheat grown in New York was not as tasty
    (b) the demand for wheat in New York was greater than the supply
    (c) Midwestern wheat was more fashionable
    (d) there were import taxes to pay

5. Improvements in farm technology in the mid-1800s meant that
    (a) planting and harvesting were done more quickly and easily
    (b) computers transformed the way the crops were grown
    (c) the farmers were soon out of jobs
    (d) most farmers went into debt buying new equipment

Lesson 12

Common Features and Patterns in Social Studies Reading

Everyday Reading

What kinds of reading do you do every day? Probably more than you think. For example, when you're waiting for dinner, you might look over the newspaper headlines or TV listings. When you're shopping or banking, you probably read signs, fliers, forms, and receipts. You may read e-mail and surf the Internet. You go to school and do homework. This all requires plenty of reading.

Social Studies Reading

When you're reading for a social studies class, you are probably not reading purely for pleasure but to gather information. How much do you know about the kinds of social studies reading your teacher assigns? How can you get the most benefit out of each kind?

Social studies reading can be divided into two basic groups: **primary sources** and **secondary sources.** Primary sources include all firsthand information: eyewitness accounts of historical events, true stories (narratives) that someone tells about his or her own life, original speeches, laws, and other firsthand official documents. Secondary sources are everything else: They are other people's versions of something that has happened.

Primary Sources

- letters
- diaries
- speeches
- government proceedings
- court testimony
- oral histories
- autobiographies

Secondary Sources

- textbooks
- news reports
- magazine or journal articles
- biographies
- histories

Both broad groups are extremely important in social studies. Textbooks and other secondary sources give you the big picture about an era or a special theme in history. Diary accounts and other primary sources give you real-life details, human emotions, and unique points of view about historical events and times. For most social studies students, though, the bulk of their reading assignments are secondary sources—textbooks and other histories.

Common Features and Patterns
in Social Studies Reading *(continued)*

Features and Patterns To Look For

Here are some of the most common features, or special characteristics, to watch for when you read social studies assignments.

Common Features

Graphics	Special Text
• maps	• bulleted/numbered lists
• charts	• boxed or shaded text
• graphs	• special chapter introductions with key topics
• time lines	• special chapter endings with summaries
• photos	• questions to think about
• drawings	• highlighted material

Each of these features needs special attention as you read. They tell you important information that regular written text cannot convey.

Here are some of the most common patterns, or ways of organizing information, to be aware of in your social studies reading.

Common Patterns

- Chronological order
- Main idea and details
- Cause and effect
- Compare and contrast

Once you learn how to recognize and interpret these features and patterns, you can apply the best possible reading strategy to each one. This will help you master social studies material. It will also help you organize and express your thoughts better when you write. In the following lessons, we'll examine many of these common features and patterns in more detail.

Lesson 13
Maps, Photos, and Drawings

Visual Literacy

In Lesson 1, graphics were referred to as "any text elements that are not just words." Graphics are information presented in various visual forms. An old saying goes, "A picture is worth a thousand words." Graphics can be very powerful. They convey a great deal of information in an efficient manner that our eyes and brains can quickly grasp.

Literacy means the ability to read and write. It also means being able to understand what you read. In the same way, students today need to be skilled in visual literacy. This means the ability to understand and interpret visual information—to "read" graphics.

Maps

In social studies, perhaps the most important and most common graphic feature is the map. Maps show, in picture form, the relative location and size of places in the world (or in the universe). Maps can describe small areas (like the layout of rooms in a museum) or large areas (like our solar system). Most often, social studies maps show important sections of our world. They may tell us about the physical world (the geography of lands and oceans, for example) or the political world (national borders, trade routes, battles fought, and so on).

To fully understand a map, it is important to be familiar with its key elements or features.

Map Features

- compass rose—indicates direction: north, south, east, west
- legend or key—explains what different markings on the map mean
- distance indicator—shows how many miles, kilometers, and so forth, a fixed distance on the map represents
- labels—words inserted on the map to indicate special places or trails, routes, and so forth
- caption—words appearing just outside the map area that tell what the whole map is showing

Maps, Photos, and Drawings *(continued)*

Photographs

When you come to a photograph in your reading, give it your full attention. Does it show something about the subject of your reading? Does it reinforce a particular theme? Or is it just decoration? Any one of these answers could be correct, depending on the reading selection.

Also consider the photographer's bias. Just as writers have personal beliefs that can color their work, so do photographers. Photos send powerful messages, but interpret them with care.

Drawings

Drawings can take many forms, including blueprints, sketches, cartoons, and diagrams, among others. In all cases, stop and look when you see a drawing in your reading selection. Interpret it as carefully as you would a photograph. What message is the drawing meant to convey?

Application

The following reading selection includes both informational text and a map. Read the selection and study the map. Use whichever graphic organizer you wish to take notes on the passage and its graphics. Then answer the questions that follow the reading.

In the early 1800s, federal policy in the United States was to absorb, or "assimilate," Native Americans. The goal was to persuade the Indians to adopt white ways of life, and to take up farming instead of roaming the land and hunting. The Shawnee chief Tecumseh called a large group together to fight assimilation and the taking of Indian lands, but they lost the struggle at the Battle of Tippecanoe. In 1828 a new president, Andrew Jackson, decided to promote an even harsher policy: removal. His Indian Removal Act of 1830 made it legal for the United States government to move all Native Americans living on eastern lands to an "Indian Territory" west of the Mississippi River.

Some tribes resisted by going to war against the whites. The Black Hawk and Seminole Wars both took place at this time. Other tribes, like the Cherokee, tried nonviolent resistance. In the end, however, all attempts to change policy failed. The Native Americans were forced to resettle in the Indian Territory set aside for them by the federal government. These trips west (see map) were long, heartbreaking, and, in many cases, deadly for these displaced native peoples.

Adapted from *Focus on U.S. History: The Era of Expansion and Reform* by Kathy Sammis. © 1997 by J. Weston Walch, Publisher.

Maps, Photos, and Drawings *(continued)*

Routes taken by Native Americans
affected by the Indian Removal Act of 1830

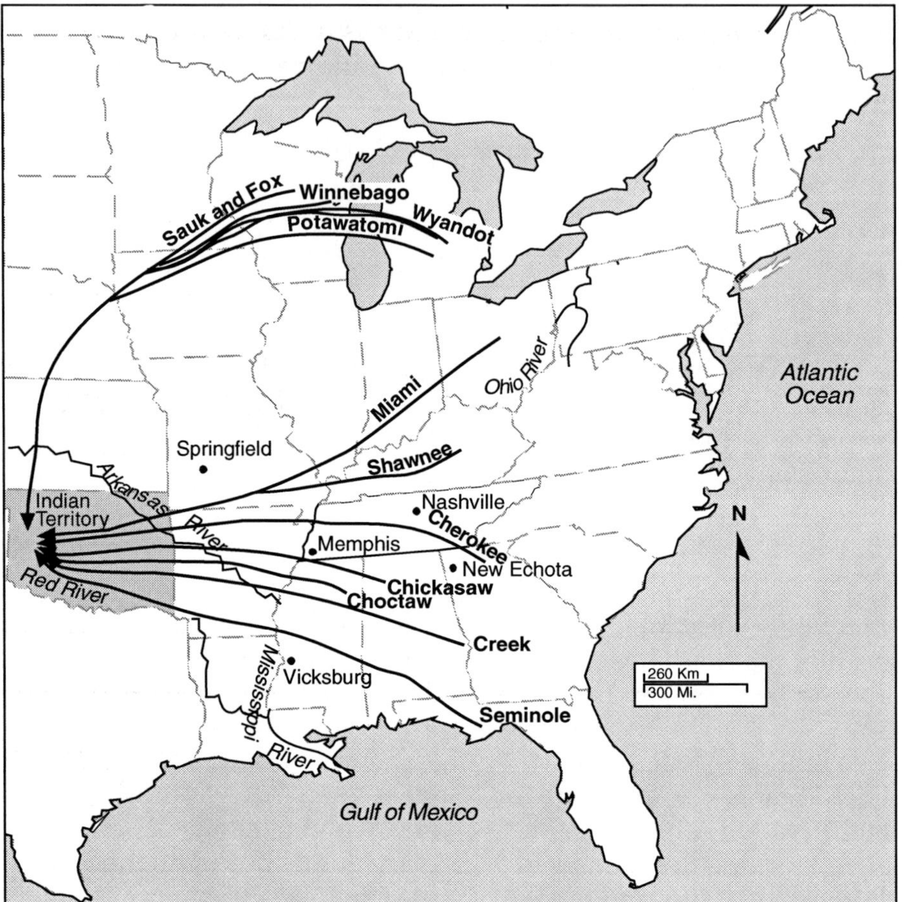

(From *Focus on U.S. History: The Era of Expansion and Reform* by Kathy Sammis, p. 100)

1. How many Native American tribes are represented on this map? _______

2. In what state(s) does the Indian Territory appear to be?

   ____

3. Most of this territory lies between what two rivers?

   ____

4. How many states were these Native American forced to leave? _______

5. About how many miles long was the trail taken by the Miami? _______

6. About how many miles long was the trail taken by the Cherokee? ______

Lesson 14
Charts, Graphs, and Time Lines

Charts, graphs, and time lines appear often in social studies reading. What do these graphic organizers look like? What purpose does each one serve?

Charts

Charts present a group of facts about a particular topic. This information takes the form of a table or other simple diagram. A typical chart looks like this.

Paper Currency: Denomination	Front	Back
1	George Washington	"One" and U.S. Seal
2	Thomas Jefferson	Monticello*
5	Abraham Lincoln	Lincoln Memorial
10	Alexander Hamilton	U.S. Treasury
20	Andrew Jackson	White House
50	Ulysses S. Grant	U.S. Capitol
100	Benjamin Franklin	Independence Hall
500	William McKinley	"Five Hundred"
1,000	Grover Cleveland	"One Thousand"
5,000	James Madison	"Five Thousand"
10,000	Salmon P. Chase	"Ten Thousand"
50,000	Carter Glass	Spread Eagle
100,000	Woodrow Wilson	"One Hundred Thousand"

* Two-dollar bills issued beginning in 1976 have a picture of the signing of the Declaration of Independence rather than a view of Monticello on the back.

In a table chart, related facts are lined up in neat columns and rows. This visual aid helps the reader sort through the information in an orderly manner. In pie charts, different facts go into different-sized wedges of the pie. In each case, the information in a chart is sorted out visually to make more sense to the reader.

Charts, Graphs, and Time Lines *(continued)*

Graphs

Graphs are special diagrams that show changes of a variable item over time. This change is usually represented by curving lines, zigzagging lines, or bars. A typical graph looks like this.

Immigration to the United States, 1800–1866

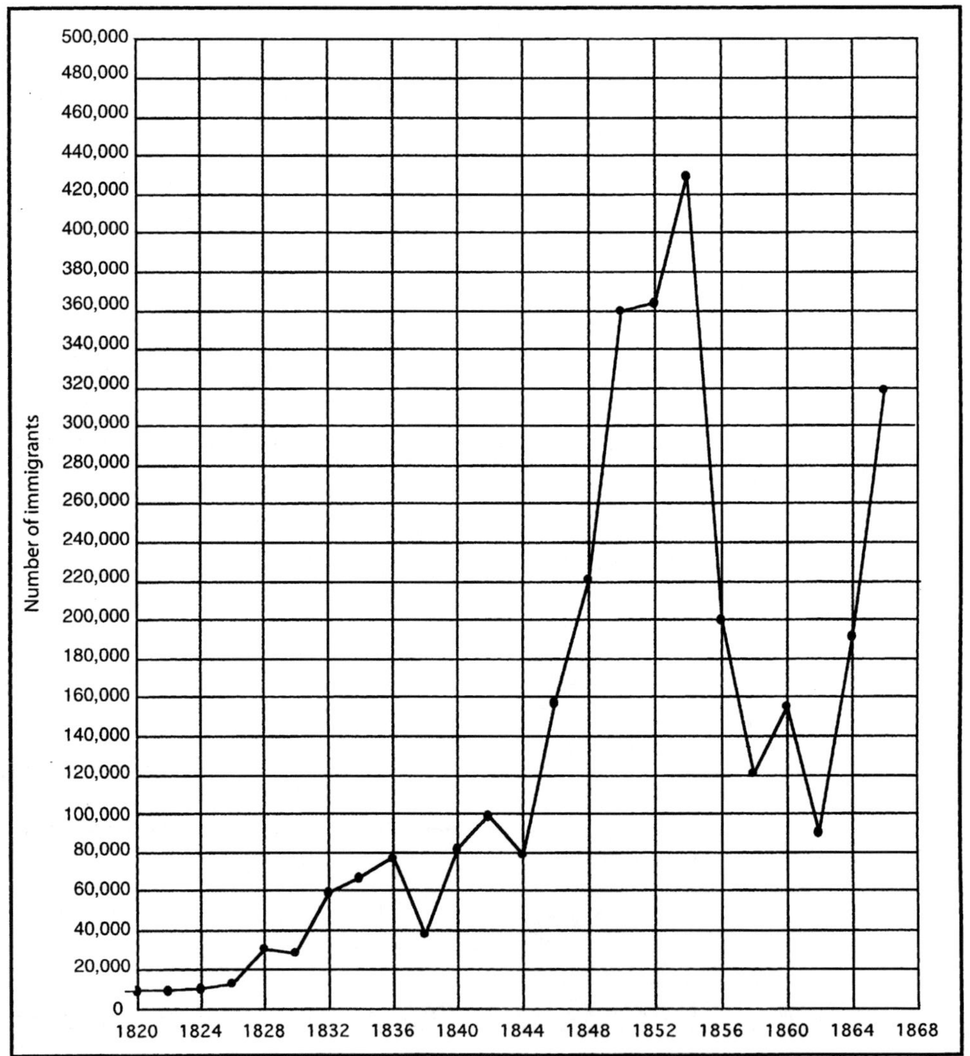

When you are reading a graph, you need to read all of the headings it contains, even if the headings are located in odd positions—like the words "Number of Immigrants" in the graph shown here. You may also need to use your index finger, a ruler, or another aid when you check the exact location of certain points on the graph line (or bar), since these points sometimes fall into "white space" on the graph (as you can see here).

Charts, Graphs, and Time Lines *(continued)*

Time Lines

The name tells it all: Time lines are graphic organizers that show time as a continuous line. Along one side of the line, important dates are noted; along the other side of the line, across from each date, a simple phrase or sentence tells what happened then. A typical time line looks like this.

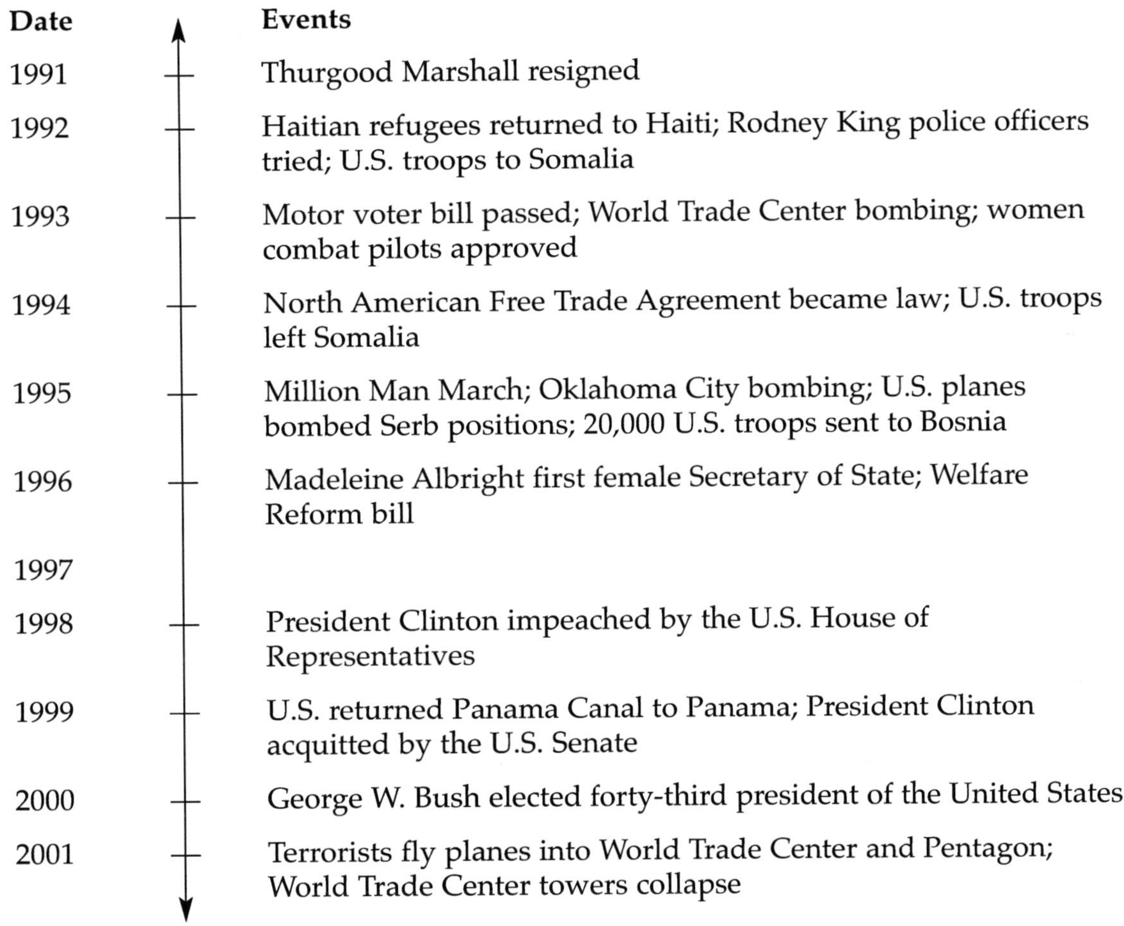

Time lines can be set up horizontally or vertically. The one shown here is arranged vertically; the time line runs up and down the page.

Charts, Graphs, and Time Lines *(continued)*

Application

The following reading selection includes both informational text and a graph. Read the selection and study the graph. Use whichever graphic organizer you like to record information from the reading and graphics. Then answer the questions that appear after the reading.

In the business world, manufacturers must constantly struggle between their desire to raise prices and the need to keep prices low enough to attract the largest number of buyers. When an item is priced too low, unit sales may skyrocket, yet the manufacturer makes less money. This is because the low price at which the product is selling does not fully cover the costs of manufacturing and advertising. On the other hand, when an item is priced too high, unit sales may plummet, yet the manufacturer makes a profit on the few items that are sold.

In the graph shown here, the solid line shows how the demand for widgets increases or decreases depending on the sales price. The dotted line shows how many widgets the manufacturer is willing to make as the sales price is increased or decreased. The point where the two lines cross is called the equilibrium market price—the point where supply and demand are in perfect balance.

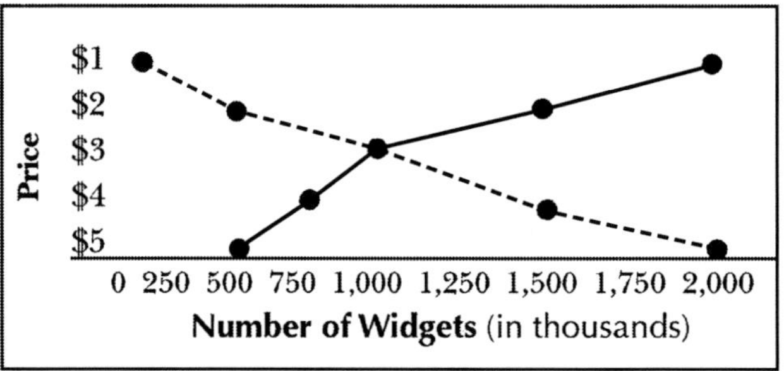

Adapted from *Understanding Our Economy* by E. Richard Churchill and Linda R. Churchill. © 1998 by J. Weston Walch, Publisher.

1. What does the dotted line on the graph show?

   ____

2. What does the solid line on the graph show?

   ____

3. The point where the two lines meet (intersect) is called what?

   ____

4. What is the ideal price for a widget, according to this graph?

   ____

5. At what point are the two lines farthest apart? Why?

   ____

Lesson 15
Chronological Order

Authors of social studies materials usually arrange their information in one of four ways. These are: (1) chronological order, (2) main idea and details, (3) cause and effect, and (4) compare and contrast. Writers will select one of these four patterns because it fits their information best and communicates their ideas most clearly.

Chronological Order

Perhaps the most straightforward of all the reading/writing patterns is chronological order. Based on two Greek words meaning "time" (*chronos*) and "speaking or reasoning" (*logikos*), chronological order lays out a series of events in the order of their occurrence. The earliest event comes first, followed by the next earliest, and so on, until the last (most recent) event is described.

Readers can learn to recognize the words and phrases that often signal chronological order. Naturally, these terms relate to time, sequence of events, or steps in a process. Here are some of the most common.

Chronological Order Words		
after	in the end	shortly thereafter
around the same time	last	simultaneously
before	later	since
during	latest	subsequently
earliest	next	succeeding (coming after)
finally	preceding (coming before)	then
first/second/third/etc.	prior to	was followed by

Application

The following selection was written to present information in chronological order. It was written by a prominent member of the community of Danvers, Massachusetts, in 1872. The writer here is giving part of the history of Danvers from his 1870s viewpoint. Read the selection, paying close attention to time and sequence words as well as dates. Then answer the questions that follow the reading.

Chronological Order *(continued)*

The shoemaking industry . . . had been planted in the place [Danvers] near the beginning of the century. Before that time, shoes had been made only for home use. But new markets were opening; and the men of Danvers had the [wisdom] and energy to enter upon them. . . . The goods were mostly made of the coarser sort, for the Southern slaves. They were sent chiefly in coasting vessels [ships]; but, during the War of 1812, they were carried . . . by horse-teams fitted out from this place. . . .

In about 1835, James Goodale, Otis Mudge, and others began then to make ladies' and children's shoes of a finer grade, sending them to Boston for distribution from that point. This was done at first on a small scale; but the business has since greatly increased. In 1854 there were in the town, within its present limits, thirty-five firms engaged in this business, making annually 1,562,000 pairs, valued at $1,072,258, and giving employment to about 2,500 persons—men and women.

The use of machinery in the work has increased year by year; though the most radical changes in this respect date from about 1860. Machines are now employed at almost every step. The manual labor required has been reduced one-half. . . . Production being also carried on with greater rapidity, the workmen are usually left without employment for considerable periods in each year. [It is hoped that] this very great evil . . . will not be permanent.

From Rice, *History of the First Parish in Danvers, 1672–1872*, pp. 142–143.

1. The following events are taken from the reading above, but they are listed out of order. Number each event in its proper sequence, following the chronological order of the reading.

    (a) _____ James Goodale and Otis Mudge began to make shoes of a finer grade.

    (b) _____ Machines were being used at every step of the shoemaking process.

    (c) _____ Shoes were made for slaves in the South.

    (d) _____ Shoes were sent by horseback rather than by ship because of war.

    (e) _____ There were 35 firms involved in the shoemaking business in Danvers.

    (f) _____ Very simple shoes were made mostly to be worn in the house.

Chronological Order *(continued)*

2. Does chronological order work well in this selection? Explain your answer.

\
\
\

3. Why do you think chronological order is used often in informational texts?

\
\
\

4. In what reading/writing situations is chronological order most appropriate?

\
\
\

5. In what reading/writing situations is chronological order not appropriate?

\
\
\

6. If you had a sequence of events to describe, but you did not want to use straight chronological order in your writing, how could you order the events instead?

\
\
\

Lesson 16
Main Idea and Details

Many social studies readings are not based on a particular sequence of events (as in chronological order). Instead, the focus may be on a special theme or subject—like America's reasons for entering World War II, social life in a frontier town, or Native American hunting techniques. In these cases, authors often choose to present their information using main idea and details.

How do you know when your reading is organized according to main idea and details? You can probably figure this out by reading the first paragraph or two and looking for a **topic sentence.** This is the sentence that spells out the topic or idea that the writer is focusing on—the main idea. Many of the surrounding sentences support this main topic or idea; they give further information about it. These are the sentences providing the details.

Topic sentence = Main idea

Supporting sentences = Details

It is important to remember that the main idea does not always come first. Often, of course, the topic sentence will appear at the very beginning of a paragraph. At other times, however, the topic sentence may be sandwiched into the middle of a paragraph, or it may appear at the end of the paragraph.

Remember, too, that there may be more than one main idea, especially if the reading passage contains more than one or two paragraphs. Generally speaking, each new paragraph introduces a new thought. Therefore, readers need to examine each paragraph to see whether it contains a brand-new topic sentence, or whether it is continuing to support the topic sentence in the preceding paragraph.

Application

The following selection presents information according to a main-idea-and-details pattern. Read the selection, looking closely for topic sentences and supporting sentences. Then answer the questions that appear after the reading.

Main Idea and Details *(continued)*

Most of the ancient Greeks worshipped the same gods (or deities). These were the gods of Mount Olympus. Yet, from town to town, there was a wide variety in the form this worship took. The Greeks had no official religious documents or books (like the Bible or the Koran). Therefore, they simply followed the religious customs of their local communities. They visited their temples as individuals, making special offerings or prayers as needed. They also celebrated together at religious festivals, which were often rather rowdy social events. In short, the Greeks had no central religious authority and no formal creed, or set of beliefs.

The ancient Greek gods were closely tied to nature and daily family life. Zeus, the king of the gods, was often considered a father figure. Poseidon ruled the oceans, making calm seas or ferocious storms for the Greek sailors to navigate. Aphrodite, goddess of love and beauty, helped—or interfered—in the romantic lives of young men and women. The wild god Pan protected the flocks of sheep and goats that many Greek families depended on for survival.

1. The following sentences can be found in the reading above. For each sentence, indicate whether it represents a main idea or a detail. Write **MI** for main idea and **D** for detail.

    (a) Yet, from town to town, there was a wide variety in the form this worship took. ________

    (b) The Greeks had no official religious documents or books (like the Bible or the Koran). ________

    (c) In short, the Greeks had no central religious authority and no formal creed, or set of beliefs. ________

    (d) Zeus, the king of the gods, was often considered a father figure. ________

    (e) Most of the ancient Greeks worshipped the same gods (or deities). ________

    (f) The wild god Pan protected the flocks of sheep and goats that many Greek families depended on for survival. ________

    (g) The ancient Greek gods were closely tied to nature and daily family life. ________

    (h) They visited their temples as individuals, making special offerings or prayers as needed. ________

Main Idea and Details *(continued)*

2. How many topic sentences did you find in this passage?

    ____

    ____

3. For each topic sentence that you identified, describe its location.

    ____

    ____

4. Which location do you prefer for a topic sentence? Why?

    ____

    ____

Lesson 17
Cause and Effect

When authors want to tell how one event in history triggered other events, or how the climate of a particular country affects its agriculture, or how high demand for a new product can create shortages and higher prices, for example, they organize their information to show cause and effect. Cause and effect shows how one condition or event results in another.

Think of a set of dominoes, standing on their ends and arranged neatly in a row. Your finger— or a gust of wind, or the wagging tail of a dog—hits the first domino in the row. It begins to fall. This is cause and effect. As it falls, the first domino hits the second one; the second domino falls, too—and then the third, the fourth, and so on down the row. This type of chain reaction—a whole series of events rather than just one—can also be shown using the cause-and-effect pattern.

Order

It is important to keep in mind that the cause does not always come first in the reading. The cause may appear in the middle or at the end of a paragraph, too. When this happens, the effects come first in the reading. You need to read through the effects to arrive at their cause.

Here are some common words and phrases to look for in a passage containing cause and effect.

Cause and Effect Words		
affect	effect	lead to
bring about	impact	result
cause	influence	trigger

Remember, there may be more than one effect for each cause. Think of the dominoes and the chain reaction. Also, there may be more than one cause. Think, for example, of World War II and the various factors that caused the United States to join that conflict.

Cause and Effect *(continued)*

Application

The following selection presents information according to the cause-and-effect pattern. Read the selection carefully. Then answer the questions that follow the reading.

In 1874 came a giant calamity in the form of a raid of grasshoppers which ate up every bit of green vegetation from the Rocky Mountains to and beyond the Missouri River. I recall that when coming home late one afternoon for supper I stepped back surprised to see what became known as Rocky Mountain locusts covering the side of the house. Already inside, they feasted on the curtains. Clouds of them promptly settled down on the whole country—everywhere, unavoidable. People set about killing them to save gardens, but this soon proved ridiculous. . . . Vast hordes, myriads. In a week grain fields, gardens, shrubs, vines, had been eaten down to the ground or to the bark. Nothing could be done. You sat by and saw everything go.

When autumn came with the country devastated, the population despaired again when seeing the insects remaining for the winter with the apparent plan of being on hand for the next season. . . .

From Stuart Henry, *Conquering Our Great American Plains.* New York: E.P. Dutton & Co., Inc. 1930. As found in Commager and Nevins, eds., *The Heritage of America,* p. 861.

1. The passage above describes the great grasshopper plague of 1874. The author has described some of the immediate effects of the grasshopper infestation. There are other effects, however, that you can probably infer (reason out) from the reading. For example, what happens when a whole year's crop is wiped out? How does that affect both the growers of the crop and the people who are expecting to buy it?

____

____

____

____

____

Cause and Effect *(continued)*

Finish the cause-and-effect chart below, adding as many effects from the reading and
from your inferences as possible.

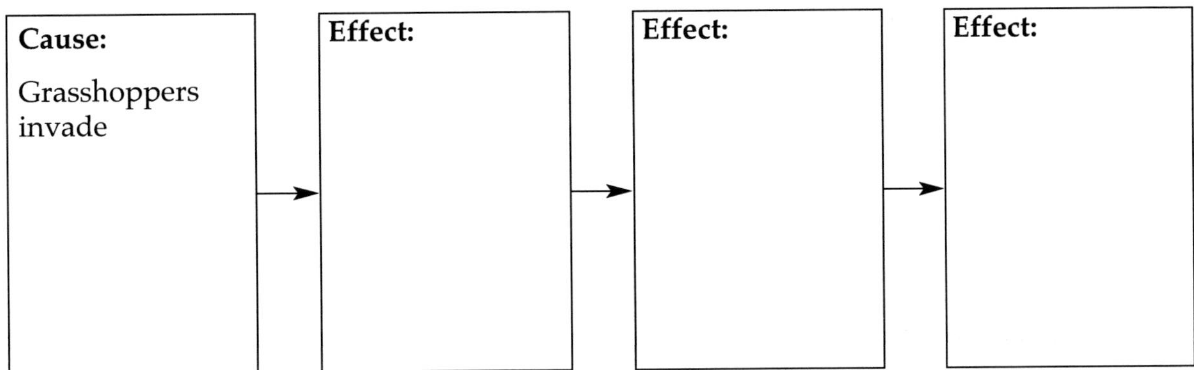

2. Does organizing information by showing cause and effect help you remember
    what you read? Why or why not?

    ____

    ____

    ____

    ____

3. Think of your social studies themes and topics at school this year. In which
    cases do you think arranging the material to show cause and effect would be
    most useful?

    ____

    ____

    ____

    ____

Lesson 18
Compare and Contrast

When we compare one person or thing with another, we are looking for ways in which they are similar. When we contrast someone or something with another, we are looking for ways in which they are different. By identifying both the similarities and the differences, we are seeing both sides of a subject, with the goal of understanding it better.

In the world of social studies, authors use comparing and contrasting as a way to organize information for many reasons, including

- to show differing beliefs or actions between key people in history
- to describe the conflicting viewpoints of two or more political groups, countries, and so on
- to relate one civilization or culture to another
- to show how something has changed over time (before/after)

Here are some common words used to compare and contrast.

Compare Words	Contrast Words
equal	contrary
identical	different/differing
in comparison	in contrast
like	on the other hand
resemble	opposite/opposing
same	unlike
similar/similarly	

Application

The following selection was written to compare and contrast information. Read the selection carefully, using a graphic organizer. Then answer the questions that follow the reading.

Compare and Contrast *(continued)*

The Anasazi culture first took root sometime around the beginning of the Common Era. These Pueblo Indian peoples inhabited what is now New Mexico and Arizona. In the one thousand years between the first and third phases of their culture, several significant developments occurred.

In their first stage of civilization, the Anasazi lived in caves or in small, round adobe huts. They hunted with flint-headed spears and grew a species of small corn for food. They wove simple baskets for containers and smoked tobacco.

Other than in winter, when they wore furs, they were naked except for sandals on their feet.

By the time of their third phase of civilization, the Anasazi lived in networks of cliff dwellings that were difficult for enemies to attack. Their buildings were terraced—much like some modern skyscrapers—and their basket weaving, now in black-on-white designs, had reached a new level of sophistication. They wove fabrics for clothing and wore jewelry made of shells, seeds, and turquoise. For weapons they now used bows and arrows.

1. Complete the graphic organizer below, using information from the reading about the Anasazi. Compare and contrast features of the first and third stages of their civilization. Two categories have been included. Add the other appropriate categories yourself.

Category	First Stage (around 1 C.E.)	Third Stage (around 1000 C.E.)
Housing		
Weapons		

2. Does organizing information in the compare-and-contrast pattern help you remember what you read?

3. Think of your social studies themes and topics at school this year. In which cases do you think comparing and contrasting would be most useful?

4. Are there other organizational patterns you might use to arrange the material in this reading about the Anasazi?

Lesson 19
Review

In the previous lessons, you have studied—and applied—some powerful new strategies to use in your social studies reading. Now, you will have the opportunity to practice these new reading strategies with some longer reading selections. First, let's review what you've learned.

The Reading Process

There are three stages in effective reading: (1) prereading, (2) reading, (3) postreading. Each of these stages involves specific steps. If you follow these steps when you read, you learn and remember much more.

Prereading (before reading) 4 Ps	Reading	Postreading (after reading)
Preview Predict Prior knowledge Purpose	**Using graphic organizers:** KWL (what I Know; what I Want to know; what I have Learned) SQ3R (Survey, Question, Read, Recall, Reflect) **Semantic web** **Outline** **Structured notes**	ALWAYS either: **Summarize** (using words from text) OR **Paraphrase** (using your own words)

Common Reading/Writing Patterns in Social Studies

Learn to recognize these patterns and you'll become a stronger, more independent reader.

Chronological Order	Main Idea/Details	Cause and Effect	Compare/Contrast
Time—events laid out in sequence, in order as they happened	**Main idea** = topic sentence **Details** = sentences that support main idea Main idea doesn't always come first in reading!	**Cause** triggers other events **(Effects).** Cause doesn't always come first in reading!	**Compare** = what's *similar* **Contrast** = what's *different* 2 or more things/people examined

Writing Strategies

Lesson 1
Writing Process Review

The Writing Process

Many people think that being a writer means putting pencil to paper or fingers to keyboard and just beginning to write. But that is not true. Writing is actually a series of steps, or a process. Every writer goes through the same process, no matter what he or she is writing. A newspaper writer, a novelist, a technical writer, a poet, and a student all go through the same steps to make their writing clear, informative, easy to read, and enjoyable.

This series of steps that writers take to put their ideas on paper is called the **writing process.** The writing process consists of four steps:

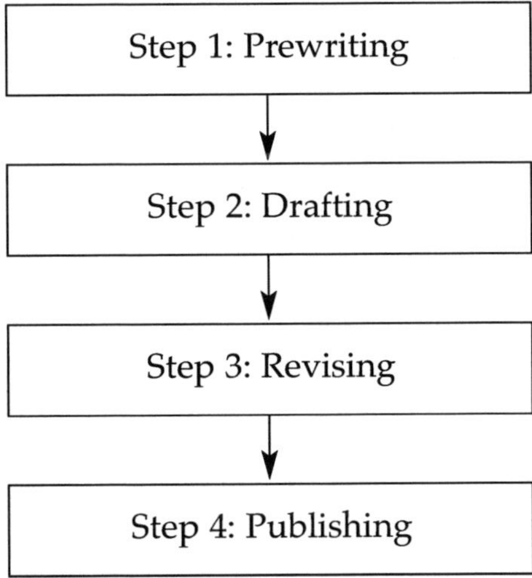

In this book, you will be exploring all four steps as well as sharpening your writing skills.

Parts of an Essay

When you have followed the writing process to write an essay, you will produce a piece that has an introduction, a body, and a conclusion. The **introduction** is the beginning of your essay. Generally, it tells what your essay will show or prove or discuss. This is where your thesis statement or topic sentence appears.

The **body** supplies the support for your thesis statement or topic sentence. It follows through on the introduction and gives the details that show your point.

Writing Process Review *(continued)*

The **conclusion** usually restates your thesis statement or topic sentence and brings the whole essay to a satisfying close.

Prewriting

The great American novelist Ernest Hemingway once wrote, "My working habits are simple: long periods of thinking, short periods of writing." For most writers, Hemingway's statement rings true: The most important part of writing really occurs **before** you begin to write.

The first step of writing is called **prewriting.** Prewriting is all the thinking and planning you do before you begin writing your first draft.

Prewriting has four steps:

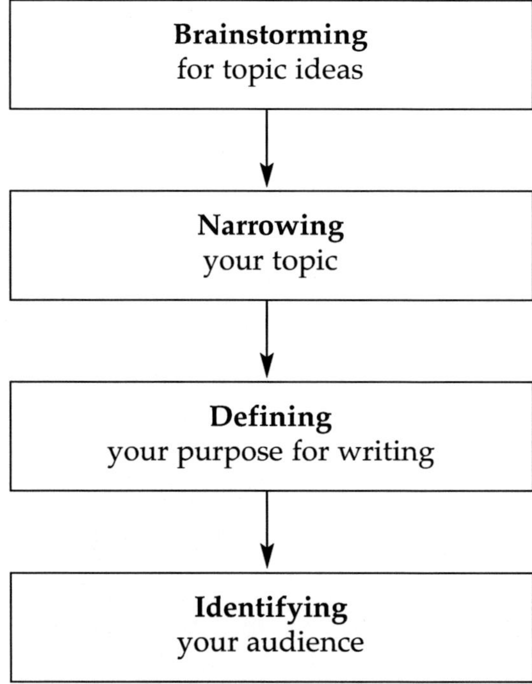

Lesson 2
Brainstorming

Have you ever brainstormed for a good idea? It's a great process—there are no rules! When you brainstorm, you think of as many things as you can about a topic without stopping to think whether they make sense or are "right." For example, let's say you want to brainstorm what you want for a birthday present. When you brainstorm, you let your mind go wherever it wants to with no "red lights," or rules to stop you.

Brainstorming Web

Brainstorming works really well when you create a web to list your ideas. Here's an example of what the web might look like for your brainstorm about birthday presents. You'll note that some things are a bit improbable for a birthday. But remember, this is the brainstorming phase, and anything goes.

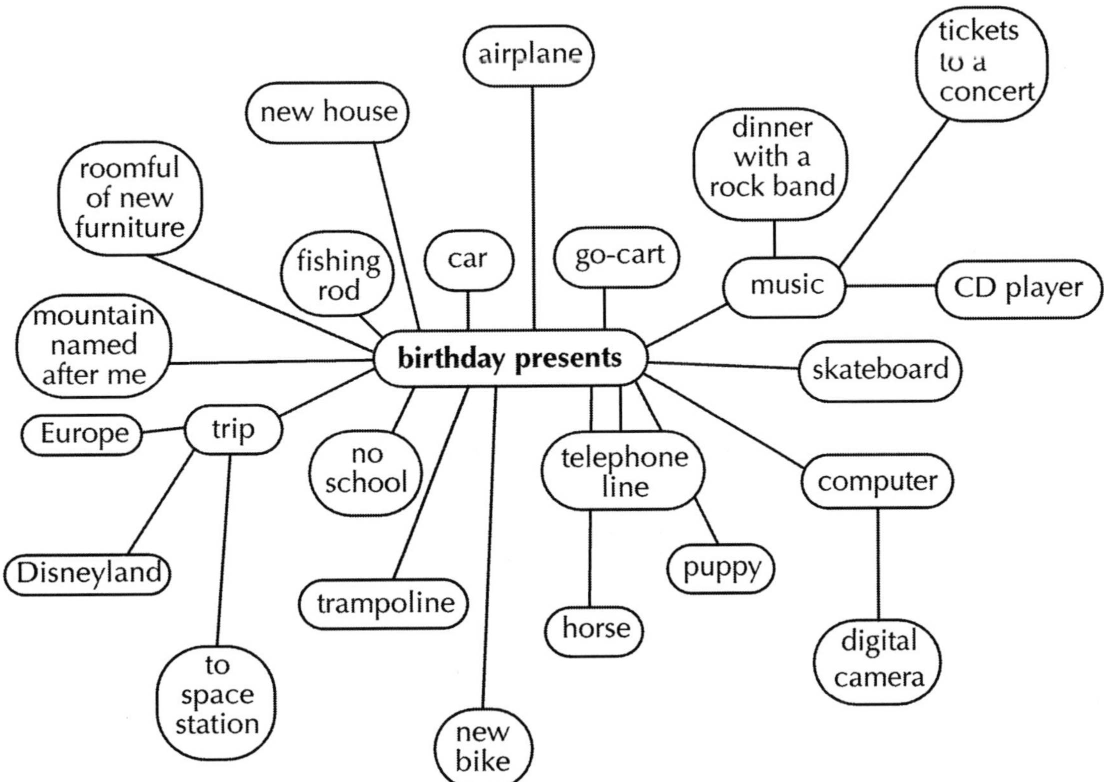

Brainstorming *(continued)*

Try It

In school, you are often asked to write about a topic either on a test or as an essay. Just as you brainstormed for what presents you might want for your birthday, you can brainstorm about the topic you are asked to write about. Let's say you've been asked the following:

Write an essay discussing the importance of space exploration in our society.

Where do you start? Use the web below to start brainstorming everything you can think of about space exploration. Don't worry about whether what you've written is "right" or not. Just write freely to discover what you know about the topic. You may not use all the spaces—or you may need to add some. You may want to remove some connecting lines, or you may want to link different boxes.

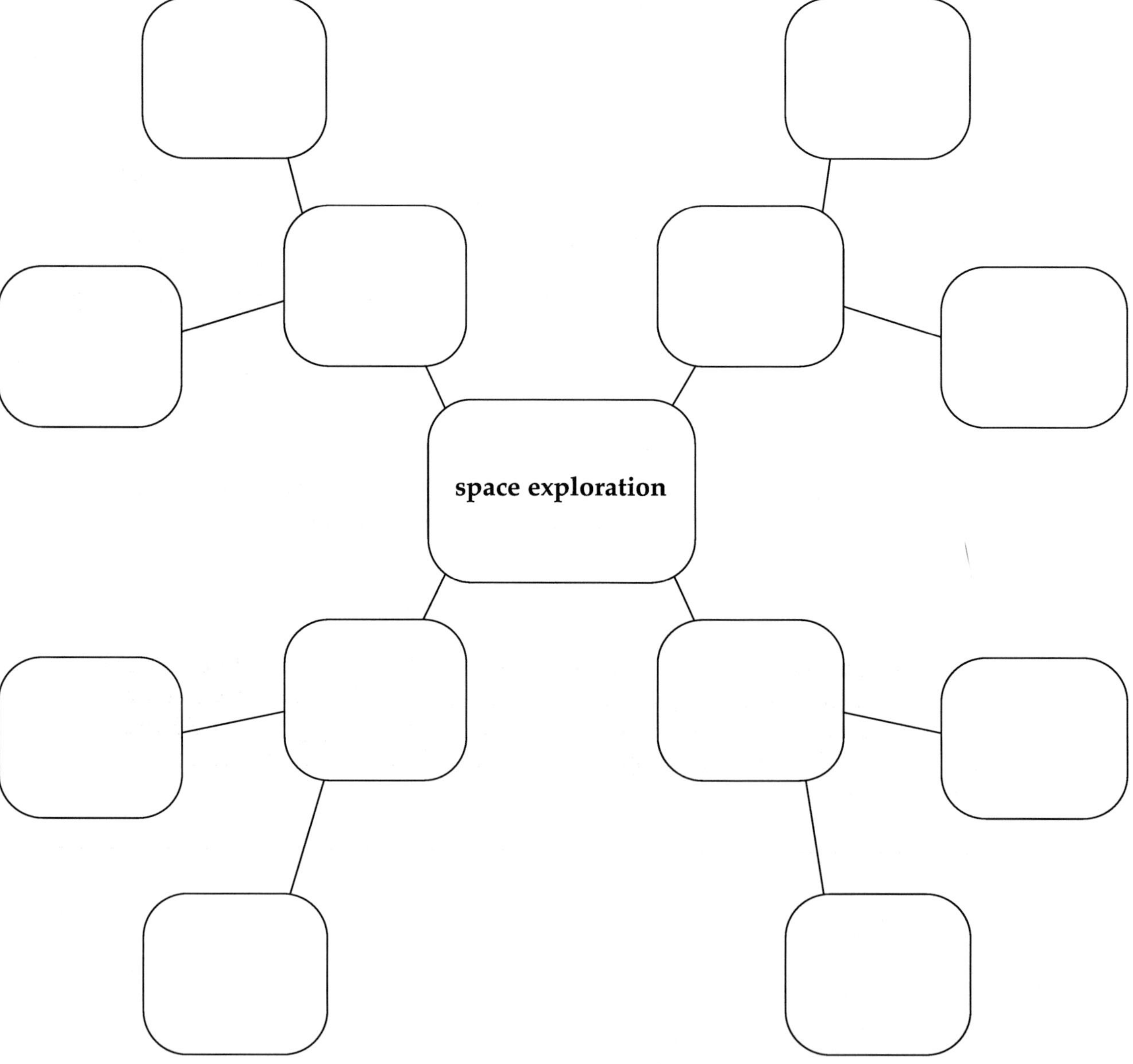

Lesson 3
Narrowing Your Topic

Analyze the Web

After brainstorming, the next phase of the prewriting or planning part of writing is to focus, or **narrow your topic.** You do this by taking a look at your brainstorming web and asking yourself three questions:

1. What part of the topic interests me the most? (What part of my web is filled in the most?)

2. What part of the topic do I know the most about?

3. What further information, if any, do I need to write about a specific aspect of the topic?

From Broad to Narrow

Let's say that you look at your web and you see that you have filled in the names of four space explorers: Sally Ride, Neil Armstrong, Christa McAuliffe, and John Glenn. You have studied them, and you know something about all of them. You could narrow your topic by writing about space explorers and their contributions to society. But would writing about all four of them be too much for your assignment? If so, then you may want to narrow your topic even further and write only about one or two of these people.

Or, let's say that you have filled in a lot of information about science-fiction movies, television shows, and books. You may want to write about how space exploration is regarded in popular culture.

Or, you may have filled in a lot of information around the topic of the Space Station. What specifically might you want to write about the Space Station?

Try It

Take a look now at what you filled in on your web about space exploration. What part interests you the most? What did you fill in the most? What do you know the most about? What will be your topic to respond to the following essay prompt: **Write an essay discussing the importance of space exploration in our society.** Write your narrowed topic here.

____

Lesson 4
Purpose

Why Are You Writing This Essay?

Now that you've narrowed your topic for writing, you need to examine what, exactly, your **purpose** is for writing. The purpose for writing is the reason you are writing. You could say that your purpose for writing is "because the teacher assigned the question." That is true, of course, but you need to look a little deeper to decide why—and how— you are going to present your topic.

People write for a number of reasons. In fiction or poetry, people write to entertain or to describe. When writing an essay, people write for the following reasons:

- to inform or explain
- to describe
- to analyze
- to persuade
- to express thoughts or opinions

Once you know your purpose for writing, you can decide what content and what language you want to use in your essay. For example, if you were writing to inform your readers about space explorers, you might be very specific about the dates, the names, and the voyages of each explorer. If you were writing to express your thoughts about space exploration, you might use opinion words like *I think, it seems, I believe . . . .*

State Your Purpose

Let's say that you wanted to pursue the idea of space explorers. Your purpose might be *to inform my readers about the voyages of John Glenn.*

Or, if you wanted to write more about science fiction and popular culture, your purpose might be *to analyze the ways popular culture represents space exploration.*

Try It

Look at your own narrowed topic about space exploration, based on your brainstorming web. Are you writing to inform or explain something? Or are you writing to describe, analyze, or express your feelings? Turn that general purpose into a specific **topic sentence,** or **thesis statement.** Take the reason you are writing, decide what you want to show in your essay, and write that in a complete sentence.

Lesson 5
Audience

Who Will Read This Essay?

The final stage of the prewriting process is determining your **audience.** Your audience means simply the people who will be reading your work.

To identify your audience, you need to ask the following questions:

- How old is my audience? Are they teachers, peers, or younger?
- What background do they have in my subject?
- Do I need to define any terms for the audience?
- What opinions are they likely to have about my topic?

Identifying your audience is important because, like the purpose, it will affect the content and the language you use in your writing. If you are writing an essay for third graders to read, you would use very different vocabulary than you would for sixth graders or for your teacher. When writing for third graders, you might write a lot more explanation about your topic. For example, let's say that you are writing about John Glenn for third graders. You cannot assume that they have heard of him. You also cannot assume that they know the word *astronaut* or even the word *orbit*—key words in describing John Glenn. For this audience, you will have to decide what words to define and what to say about John Glenn. You also need to think about what interests them. If you were writing about John Glenn for your teacher, you would assume that she or he would know words like *orbit* and *shuttle* and would have some opinions or information about your topic.

Considering Your Audience

When you are asked to write an essay for school, you can usually assume that you are writing for your teacher or for your peers. Your teacher will generally tell you if you are to write for a different audience. But remember, in any writing that you do, you need to think about what your audience already knows and what vocabulary they may or may not know.

Try It

Now think about your own topic about space exploration. Who is your audience?

____

How will your audience affect your writing?

____

____

Lesson 6
Drafting

The First Draft

Now that you've learned about the very important first step in the writing process—prewriting—it's time to put pencil to paper (or fingers to keyboard) and begin the actual writing. This second step in the writing process is called **drafting.** Drafting is when you put your prewriting ideas onto paper in complete sentences. Almost all writers create more than one draft—usually several—of their writing. The first draft is usually fairly rough. The final draft is the draft they are ready to publish, or share with others.

The first draft of your writing is where you begin to organize your writing. It is very important that your essay is organized so that it is clear and easy to understand. You want to be sure your facts are right and that you back them up with supporting evidence. You want to be sure that your readers can follow your logic and the order of events. You want to be sure that it is clear what the main points are. And, you want to be sure that your writing is believable.

Common Patterns in Social Studies

Most writing in the social studies area is organized in a pattern that is easy to identify and easy to re-create. These patterns show logical order, illustrate the main ideas, or analyze the causes of certain events.

Four of the most common patterns you'll find in social studies reading are as follows:

- **chronological order:** This is a pattern organized by dates or by logical steps.
- **main idea and details:** This pattern tells about main events, ideas, or people and is backed up, or supported, by details to prove or show examples of the main idea.
- **cause and effect:** This pattern explains why or how an event or a condition came to be.
- **compare and contrast:** This pattern shows how one event, person, or idea is like or unlike another.

Lesson 7
Chronological Order

Have you ever had someone give you directions—in the wrong order? What happens? You get lost! Or, has someone ever described an event and told the details all out of order? What happens then? You find it very hard to follow the story.

In social studies and history, a common organizational pattern in writing is called **chronological order.** This pattern shows how events are lined up in time sequence. A timeline is a great graphic representation of chronological order. A biography is another example: It tells about a person's life from one point of time (usually birth) through another point in time (usually death). Sometimes in history and social studies, you'll read about events that take place in **sequential order.** This pattern is similar to chronological order in that it tells how things happen in a logical sequence, usually steps of a process. A set of directions from one place to another is a great example of sequence. A cookbook is full of writing in sequential order—each recipe gives the logical order of steps to prepare a meal.

Good Writing Tip: Use Chronological Order Words

Chronological and sequential order are easy to recognize in your social studies reading. Often you can recognize this pattern because you'll see dates listed. You'll also see key words that tell you this pattern is being used. Some common chronology and sequence words follow. Use words like these when you write in the chronological order pattern. They will help your reader keep track of what happens when.

Chronological Order Words			
after	following	meanwhile	soon
also	fourth	new	then
begin	in (date or time)	next	third
earlier	in addition to	now	today
end	last	old	tomorrow
finally	later	second	too
first			

Chronological Order *(continued)*

Model

Look at the paragraphs below. Carefully scan them for chronology words. Notice how the ages of history are described in logical, chronological order.

The Tools of History

Historians have long identified periods of early history by the tools humans used to cultivate their lives. The first of the "tool" ages was called the Stone Age. It is said to have begun when humans first used tools—around 2.5 million years ago—and extended to 8,000 B.C.E.

The next phase of history were known as the metal ages. These ages were named after whatever metal was predominantly used for tools in place of stone. The first of these ages was called the Copper Age; it began around 8,000 B.C.E. and continued through 2,000 B.C.E. Next came the Bronze Age, which overlapped the Copper Age, and is thought to have begun as early as 2,500 B.C.E. It was followed by the Iron Age, which continued from 2,500 B.C.E. through the Middle Ages to around 1700 C.E.

The metal ages began to wane around 1700 C.E. At that time in Europe and in North America, a new age—the Industrial Age—began. This age is marked by the use of complex machinery. Today we are living at the end of the Industrial Age. A new age is just beginning. What do you think our new age is being called? What is the dominant tool of the twenty-first century?

What clues from "The Tools of History" tell you that this article is organized in a chronological pattern? First, notice that there are dates throughout the paragraphs. These dates are in chronological order. (This one is a bit tricky, because you need to know that B.C.E. time works backwards up to 1 C.E.) Then look for some chronology words. In the first paragraph, there is one key word: *first*. In the second paragraph, there are several: *next, first, next, followed by*. In the third paragraph, there are three words that give you clues that the article is written in chronological order: *new, began,* and *today*.

Try It

Read the following "notes" of Sir Brag of Joustalot about becoming a knight. Even though this article is written in the first person, it contains important chronological facts about becoming a knight. Keep a lookout for the key words that help you understand the sequence of becoming a knight.

Chronological Order *(continued)*

"How I Became a Knight"—notes of Sir Brag of Joustalot

This isn't easy, this becoming a knight business. Believe me, I know about it firsthand. There's a lot to it—lots of things I have to do and missions I have to accomplish. Here's a breakdown of some of what I had to do, in case you were thinking of becoming a knight.

The first thing I had to do was be born a boy. The second thing I had to do was be born rich with a lot of land. Those were the easy parts. From then on, it was practice, practice, practice.

When I turned six, I officially became a page. This meant that I had to leave home and move to a castle far away to serve its lord and lady. I had to learn good manners and to be obedient. Sometimes that part was boring, but I knew it was important because knights have to be ultrapolite. The best part of being a page was that I got to learn how to use a sword, and that was a lot of fun. I got to practice with a lot of other guys who were hoping to become knights one day, too.

Then, when I turned 14, I became a squire. My job was to help a knight prepare for battle. I was in charge of my knight's armor and all his weapons. (They were very heavy!) I had to polish the weapons and make sure that all the metal on the knight's armor was strong and well fortified. Every once in a while, I would go with my knight into battle. This was good, because the only way I could get to be a real knight was to experience warfare for four whole years. Sometimes it took longer, like for me. It took me eight years to qualify to be a knight.

Finally, the day came for me to become a knight. The night before I stayed up holding vigil, which means I prayed all night to be a good knight. The next day—the big day—I was pretty nervous. I walked into the queen's chambers (if you've got a king, then it's the king who does it) and she dubbed me, which means she tapped me first on my right shoulder with a sword and then on my left. Then she gave me my title, and I got a new sword and a special set of spurs made out of gold.

Now that I am a knight, I have to support myself and an army of soldiers. Now it's my turn to help other worthy squires train to become great soldiers and ultimately knights like me.

Chronological Order (*continued*)

Put the events below in chronological order, according to the reading passage on page 101. Number the events from 1 to 8.

___ Brag practices swordplay.

___ Brag becomes a squire.

___ Brag is dubbed a knight.

___ Brag follows his knight into battle.

___ Brag moves to a castle far from home.

___ Brag trains other squires how to be knights.

___ Brag holds an all-night vigil.

___ Brag becomes a page.

Look again at the article about Sir Brag becoming a knight. Circle the chronological or sequential order words.

Application

Now it's your turn to try your hand at writing using chronological order. Below is a list of possible writing topics. All of them are related to the articles that follow on great moments in baseball history. Select the topic that most interests you. Then follow the steps in the writing process to make your essay the best it can be.

1. Imagine that you are explaining the three historic baseball moments in a letter to a friend who has never seen a baseball game. How will you describe these three events?

2. Role-play you are a baseball announcer giving a play-by-play description of one or two of the baseball moments in the articles that follow. How will you tell about the game to your listening fans?

3. Describe a memorable sports moment that you have experienced either as a player or as a spectator. Explain what made the game or the moment special.

Chronological Order *(continued)*

The Shot Heard 'Round the World

It's rare that New York plays New York in a playoff for the National League pennant, but that's what happened on October 3, 1951. The New York Giants and the Brooklyn Dodgers faced off at the Polo Grounds in New York for a dramatic ending in the pennant race. The Giants had trailed the Dodgers all season—only two months before the playoff game, they were behind 13 1/2 games.

The moment most baseball historians consider the number-one moment in all baseball history is referred to as "The Shot Heard 'Round the World." This phrase refers to the expression used to mark the start of the American Revolution. It describes a "revolution" in the history of baseball.

The Giants' Bobby Thomson was at bat. The score was 4–1, with Brooklyn leading. It didn't look good for the Giants: It was the bottom of the ninth inning, which meant the last possible moment of the game. Brooklyn had the game—and the pennant—practically won.

Early in the bottom of the ninth, the Giants scored one more run. Now the score was 4–2. Then Thomson came up to bat. There were Giants' runners at second and third. The Brooklyn manager brough Ralph Branca in to pitch against Thomson. The crowd was anxiously beginning a low roar.

Branca pitched the first ball to Thomson. Swing and a miss. Strike one. Then Branca pitched him a second ball. It was a fastball, high and inside. The umpire would have called it a ball. Instead, Thomson swung the bat and cracked the ball, sending it hurtling five rows deep into the stands. Runners came screeching home from second and third while Thomson loped around the bases. "We beat 'em, we beat 'em," he kept saying to himself as he rounded the bases. Later he said, "I felt like I was floating, like my feet weren't touching the ground." The Giants won, 5–4, then went on to lose the World Series. No one remembers that loss; they only remember the stunning moment of "the shot heard 'round the world."

Chronological Order *(continued)*

Independence Day for the Luckiest Man

Lou Gehrig is considered one of baseball's greatest players. That's why on July 4, 1939, his appearance at Yankee Stadium in New York was a moment that went down in history.

Gehrig had just completed a streak of 2,130 games played. He was at the absolute top of his game when he was diagnosed with a rare and debilitating neurological disease called amyotrophic lateral sclerosis. There is no cure for ALS.

To honor Gehrig, the Yankees held Lou Gehrig Appreciation Day on July 4. The Seventh Regiment Band played and escorted the most glittering of baseball stars to home plate: Babe Ruth, Bobby Meusel, Tony Lazzeri, Mark Koenig, Waite Hoyt, Herb Pennock, and Wally Pipp. This group was soon joined by the New York Yankees and the New York Senators, who stood behind the microphone at home plate. The crowd began to chant, "We want Lou, we want Lou, we want Lou."

Gehrig was then escorted out of the dugout to receive tributes, trophies, speeches, poems, more music, and thunderous applause. Soon an awkward silence fell over the stadium. It was Gehrig's turn to talk, but he was so moved, so touched by the tribute, that he found himself unable to speak. He whispered to master of ceremonies Sid Mercer that he wouldn't be able to give his speech after all. Said Mercer, "Ladies and gentlemen, Lou Gehrig has asked me to thank you all for him. He is too moved to speak."

But the fans wouldn't let Gehrig stay silent. They began their chant again, "We want Lou, we want Lou!"

Gehrig wiped his eyes, blew his nose, and walked slowly toward the microphone. There he made the speech that made baseball history:

"Fans, for the past two weeks you have been reading about a bad break I got. Yet today I consider myself the luckiest man on the face of the earth. I have been in ballparks for 17 years and have never received anything but kindness and encouragement from you fans. Look at these grand men. Which of you wouldn't consider it the highlight of his career just to associate with them for even one day? . . .

". . . Sure I'm lucky. When the New York Giants, a team you would give your right arm to beat, and vice versa, sends you a gift—that's something! When everybody down to the groundskeepers and those boys in white coats remember you with trophies—that's something . . . !

". . . When you have a wonderful mother-in-law who takes sides with you in squabbles against her own daughter—that's something! When you have a father and mother who work all their lives so that you can have an education and build your body—it's a blessing! When you have a wife who has been a tower of strength and shows more courage than you dreamed existed—the finest I know . . ."

". . . So I close in saying that I might have been given a bad break, but I have an awful lot to live for! Thank you."

Chronological Order *(continued)*

Breaking the World Record

"I remember talking to reporters before the game and saying, 'You know what? Somebody needs to tell this guy that he's about to break the most prestigious record in sports history, because it's like he doesn't even know it.' "—St. Louis Cardinals backup catcher Tom Lampkin

The day was September 8, 1998. The place was Busch Stadium, in St. Louis, Missouri. The game was sold out. The crowd had come to see if Mark McGwire would break the biggest record in baseball history: hitting more than 61 home runs in a single season. The record had been set by Roger Maris in 1961. Now, 37 years later, McGwire stood to break the record.

McGwire walked the first time he was up in the game. Then, in the fourth inning, he hit Chicago's Steve Trachsel's first pitch and sent it quickly flying over the left field wall before he could even leave the batter's box.

McGwire was so excited he leapt into the arms of the Cardinals' first-base coach, but forgot to touch the base! Dave McKay, the Cardinals' coach, had to push him back onto the base to make sure the play was legal.

The drama of McGwire's home-run record didn't end with this game against the Chicago Cubs. During the same season, Cubs player Sammy Sosa was vying for the same record. He hit his own number 62 with two weeks left to play in the season. For a while the two were tied for the record. No one knew who would walk away with the record at the end of the season.

The final weekend of the baseball season was tense. McGwire and Sosa were tied, now with 65 home runs apiece.

On September 25, Sosa hit a home run, pushing the record to 66 against McGwire's 65. On the same day, just an hour later, McGwire hit his 66th home run. Both players had just two more games to play. Sosa missed his chance during these games, but McGwire hit home runs twice in each of the two games. He finished the season with a huge record breaker—a 70-home-run season.

Chronological Order (*continued*)

Prewriting

Look back at the topic questions on page 102. Choose the topic that most interests you and that you feel you can write most comfortably about.

Brainstorm

Begin your written answer by using step one of the writing process—brainstorming. Use the web below to help you think of ideas for your topic. Remember, the brainstorming part of the process is the time for you to go wild with your responses and thoughts about the topic. Change the web as needed.

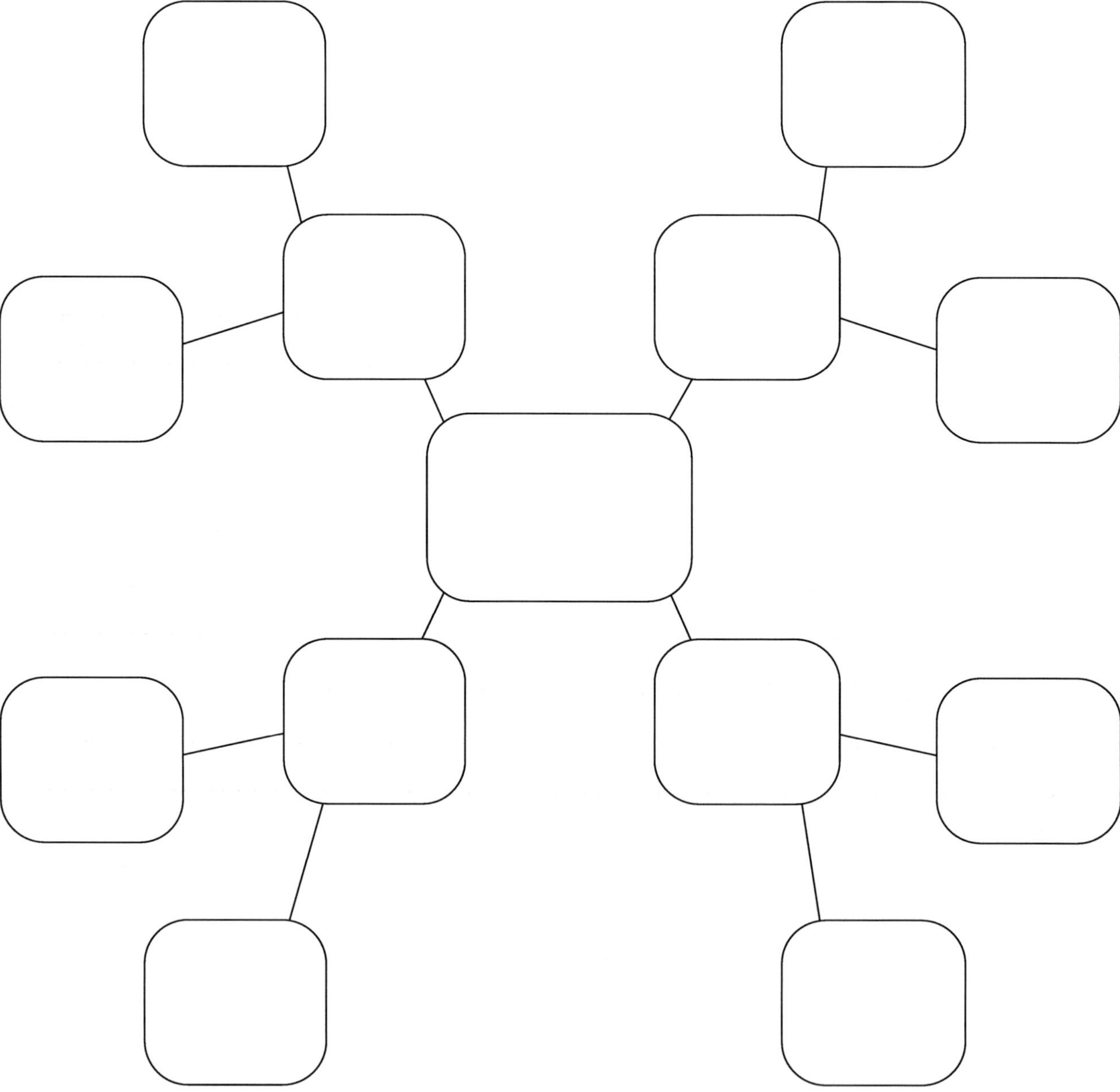

Chronological Order *(continued)*

Narrow Your Topic

Now that you have brainstormed the topic, narrrow it down. Remember to ask yourself three questions to help you narrow your topic:

- What part of the topic interests me the most? (What part of my web is filled in the most?)
- What part of the topic do I know the most about?
- What further information do I need to write my essay?

Write your narrowed topic. ____

Define Your Purpose

It's time to clarify your purpose for writing. Are you writing to inform or explain? Are you writing to describe or analyze? Or are you writing to persuade or express your own opinion or thoughts? Here's a great hint to help you define your purpose: Look for the words *explain, describe, analyze, what do you think* in the body of the essay question. Finding these words will often help you define your purpose.

What is your purpose for writing your essay? Write your purpose as a complete sentence that tells what your essay will show.

____

____

Identify Your Audience

Before you begin drafting, think for a moment about your audience—the people who will read your essay. Who is your audience?

____

____

How does this particular audience affect how you will write?

____

____

Chronological Order *(continued)*

Drafting

Now that you've done the prewriting thinking and planning, it's time to start writing. As you remember, this is a time to practice writing in the pattern called chronological or sequential order. You can use the chart below to help you organize your writing.

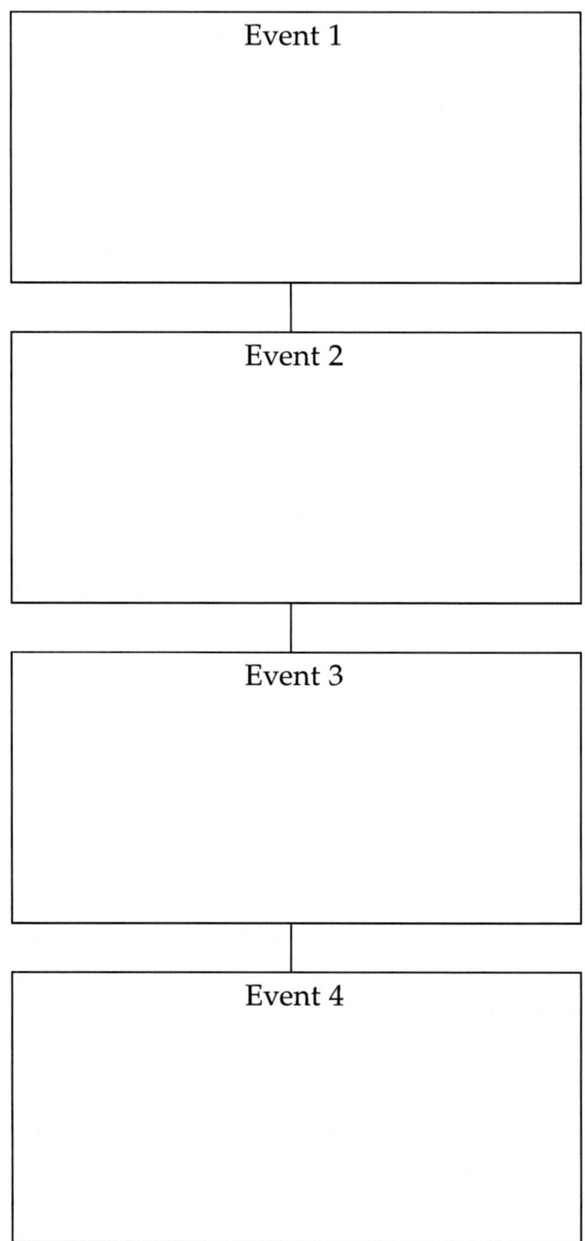

On a separate sheet of paper, begin the first draft of your essay on the topic you chose. Remember, this is a first draft—it's the place to get organized. Don't worry yet about spelling or punctuation. That comes in the next phase of the writing process.

Chronological Order *(continued)*

Revising

The word *revising* means "seeing again." When writers revise, they "see their writing again" from a fresh perspective. Sometimes writers need to "sleep" on their work. Other times they need a little help from their writer friends or a teacher to help them see what needs to be changed.

Don't be fooled into thinking that your first draft is the last draft. Revising is an integral part of writing. The writer Dorothy Canfield said, "Very young writers often do not revise at all. . . . They are hypnotized by what they have written." Canfield was not necessarily referring to writers' ages! There are very old writers who are "young" at their craft and don't understand the value of revising! Now is the best time to learn how to revise.

When you revise your draft, you need to step back and look at the big picture. Do you need to cross anything out? Do you need to add anything?

Below you'll find a series of questions that you can ask yourself. Your teacher can provide a revising checklist that includes questions like these.

- Did I state the main idea clearly?
- Have I supported the main idea with specific details, examples, and facts?
- Did I present my ideas in some kind of logical order?
- Have I written any sentences that stray from the main idea?
- Are my words specific?
- Is my purpose clear?
- Are my vocabulary and content appropriate for my audience?

Peer Editing

Conferencing is another great way to revise your work. You can choose to conference with a classmate or with a teacher. When you conference, you can ask another person to look over your work and help you with suggestions for revising. In peer conferences, you can help others with their work while they help you with yours. Your teacher can provide you with a peer-editing form.

Take time now to revise your essay about baseball moments. Use your revision questions or invite a classmate or group of classmates to help. Write your second draft using the revisions you have chosen. Check for chronology words to be sure you have used this pattern in your writing.

Chronological Order *(continued)*

Proofreading

You're almost there! You have made the big revisions to your essay. Now you need to check for the smaller problems—you need to proofread. This is where you polish your writing, checking for mechanical errors. Mechanical errors include things like typos, misspellings, bad grammar, and incorrect punctuation. Your teacher can provide you with a proofreading checklist. Once you have completed this process, your work is ready to publish, or share with your teacher or classmates.

Publishing

Write the final draft of your essay following your teacher's guidelines. Be sure that the final draft is free of mistakes and is clear, clean, and easy to read. Create an interesting title.

Lesson 8
Main Idea and Details

Main Idea Versus Details

Have you ever listened to a friend tell a story when you've waited patiently to detail after detail until you wanted to scream, "Get to the point!"? It can drive you crazy when you have no idea what the point, or main idea, of your friend's story is.

Have you ever experienced this same feeling when you are reading—or writing—something? Nothing is more frustrating than not being able to follow an essay's point. One of the most important organizational patterns in writing is called **main idea and details.** This means writing to be sure that the main point of what you want to say is clear. It also means that the main idea is fully supported by details—examples, facts, figures, names, dates, or events—to illustrate the main idea.

You use the main-idea-and-details pattern when your purpose is to explain, persuade, or inform your reader. You use it most often when you analyze an idea or explain an important point. You can also use it when you want to present a point of view and persuade your reader by adding up the details, or facts, to prove that point.

When you write, more often than not, the main idea is expressed in a **topic sentence.** This sentence often comes at the beginning of your essay, in the introductory paragraph, and can sometimes be the first sentence. In this way, it serves as the introduction to the entire essay. The topic sentence serves two purposes:

- It explains the main idea.
- It tells or implies the purpose for writing (to explain, persuade, or inform).

The details are then drawn out in the body, the paragraphs that follow the introduction. These details are facts, figures, events, stories, or examples that prove or illustrate the main idea. The details are the *who, what, where, when,* and *why* that explain the main idea.

Main Idea and Details *(continued)*

Model

Look at the paragraphs that follow. Notice how the main idea is made very clear in the first, or introductory, paragraph.

The Internet Celebrates Middle Age

Most people think that the Internet was born at the end of the twentieth century. But in reality, the Internet has been around since the late 1960s. *(Here is the topic sentence. It shows you the main idea of the article. It tells you that the Internet is older than you think. It suggests that the points that follow will explain or prove the main idea.)*

At first, the Internet was used by a small group of people. The Internet was created by the Advanced Research Projects Agency, a group that is a part of the federal government's Department of Defense. The members of this agency were scientists and scholars, and they used the Internet for a very practical purpose—to share their scientific research. *(Here are details that illustrate or explain the main idea.)*

It wasn't long before these clever researchers realized that the technology they had invented could be expanded for use by everyone— for research and for communication. By the spring of 1998, an estimated 50 million users were surfing the information highway. From then on, it is estimated that Internet traffic doubled every 100 days!

Most people would say that the Internet is still in its infancy. But those who remember know that it all began over 30 years ago. However, the Internet continues to grow, and we have yet to see its full maturity. *(Notice how the last paragraph, or conclusion, restates the main idea from the introductory paragraph.)*

Try It

Read the following article about civil disobedience. Look for the main idea and the details that support the main idea. Notice how the article is structured: the first paragraph—the introductory paragraph—introduces the main idea. The middle paragraphs—the body—show the *who, what, where, why,* and *when* details. The last paragraph—the conclusion—pulls the subject all together again and restates the main idea.

Main Idea and Details *(continued)*

A Quiet Revolution

Throughout history, people have disagreed strongly with their governments over policies, laws, and actions. In some cases, when they disagree, people write letters to their representatives. In other cases, people stage violent revolutions, as the American colonists did in 1775 and the French peasants did in 1789. But in 1849, Henry David Thoreau wrote an essay called "Civil Disobedience," which gave a name to a form of protest that would influence world events forever more.

Civil disobedience is a revolution that does not call for battles or weapons or bloodshed. Instead, it is a form of protest that invites citizens to withdraw their cooperation with their government or to stand up against injustice. This means that those practicing civil disobedience might stop obeying the law they disagree with. It might mean demonstrating in a quiet but powerful way to protest the law or policy. Or, it could mean boycotting government-funded agencies so that they are not able to run.

Two of the most famous followers of Thoreau's ideas on civil disobedience are Mohandas K. Gandhi and Dr. Martin Luther King, Jr. Both men staged quiet protests against prejudice and intolerance that were allowed by law and felt throughout society. Gandhi successfully staged a protest against the poor treatment of immigrant Indians in South Africa. As a result, laws were changed that gave Indians many more opportunities in that society. Gandhi later used the same approach against the British government in India. This helped end British control. Dr. Martin Luther King, Jr. staged nonviolent protests against laws that allowed African Americans to be banned from public places, education, or even sitting where they chose on city buses. His nonviolent actions led to the passage of new laws that opened up educational and social opportunities to African Americans.

The actions of Mohandas Gandhi and Dr. Martin Luther King, Jr. have proved that civil disobedience is a form of protest that works and can effect change. But civil disobedience requires a lot of patience. It means spending a lot of time quietly, passively resisting. This can be hard for people who want to see change happen quickly. Often people feel angry about the injustice or law they disagree with and want to see things change immediately. Civil disobedience takes discipline. It is hard work. However, many feel that it is worth the effort and time because it is done peacefully, without bloodshed. Also they feel that the time it takes to effect the change helps those who are content with the laws as they were to understand and subscribe to the changes.

As a result of civil disobedience, laws can change and lives can be transformed. Little did Thoreau know back in 1849 that his words would influence an entire century of change. Undoubtedly his essay will inspire other leaders in the years to come.

Main Idea and Details (continued)

1. What is the main idea of "A Quiet Revolution"?

   ____

2. What is the topic sentence?

   ____

   ____

3. What are four supporting details?

   ____

   ____

   ____

   ____

Good Writing Tip: Show Each Detail

Each body paragraph should show one supporting detail or idea. This is a good rule to follow to keep things organized. That way, one idea can be fully developed.

Good Writing Tip: Use Transitions

The change from one paragraph to another signals a transition from one idea to the next. Supporting paragraphs are linked through words that form a bridge or a **transition** from one idea to the next.

Often transitions are signaled by the use of words that link ideas. These words can show how things are alike or different. They can add additional information about the main idea as well. Such words can also signal the conclusion of the article. And they wrap up all the details and sum up the main idea at the end of the article. Here are some examples of transition words:

- to show how things are alike or different: *on the other hand, additionally, similarly, also, as well as, like, but*
- to further explain the main idea: *additionally, another, as well as, besides, in addition to, not only, further, before long, for example*
- to conclude or wrap up the details: *in conclusion, so, therefore, it is clear to see, clearly, understandably, in closing, never before*

Look at the article on page 112, "The Internet Celebrates Middle Age." Write the transition words or signals that tell you that the article is changing from one idea to the next.

   paragraph 1: ____

   paragraph 2: ____

   paragraph 3: ____

   paragraph 4: ____

Main Idea and Details *(continued)*

Application

Now it's your turn to try your hand at organizing an essay using main idea and details. Below is a list of possible writing topics. All of them are related to the articles that follow about flags. Select the topic that most interests you. Then follow the steps in the writing process to make your essay the best it can be.

1. "I am what you make me: nothing more. I swing before your eyes as a bright gleam of color, a symbol of yourself."—Franklin K. Lane

   Franklin K. Lane was the secretary of the interior of the United States when he spoke "for" the American flag in 1914. What does the American flag symbolize to you? What "symbol of yourself" does it represent?

2. In several countries, including the United States, there are strict rules to be followed when handling the flag. Why do you think there are rules and etiquette to flag handling? What do these rules really represent?

3. Imagine that you have been asked to redesign the American flag. What emblem would you choose for the flag? What colors would you choose? Whose advice would you seek and what criteria would you use as you make your final design choices?

Main Idea and Details *(continued)*

A Beginner's Look at Vexillology

Are you a vexillophile? There are thousands of them in the United States alone, and you may well be one. If you are a vexillophile, you are interested in vexillology. And if you are interested in vexillology, this means that you love to study—flags!

Vexillology is not a simple subject. Embedded in many of the world's flags are centuries of meaning, geography, and history. Many flags have common themes or belong to flag "families," and can tell you much about the history and even the culture of the country. For example, Ethiopia is one of the few African countries that did not experience a history of colonization by Europeans. As a result, Ethiopia was seen as a leader or a model for many emerging African nations in the 1950s and 1960s. Ethiopia's tricolor—green, yellow, and red—became a symbol for Pan-Africanism, or national unity among many African countries and their people worldwide. Ghana adopted the flag colors in 1957 and added a black star to represent its people. After that, red, yellow, green, and black became the basis for several African nations including Congo, Senegal, Rwanda, Mali, and Togo.

Islamic colors and symbols dominate the flags of North Africa and the Middle East. Green is considered a color of Allah. Many flags of Muslim countries show the crescent and star, which symbolize Hagar, the mother of Ishmael, an ancestor of Muhammad. Libya, Mauritania, and Saudi Arabia are countries where the crescent and star appear.

Cuba, Puerto Rico, Panama, and Chile all incorporate stars and stripes in their designs. These countries were influenced by the United States' fight for independence. They hoped to express their support of the United States by incorporating these elements in their flags. The Cuban and Puerto Rican flags are almost exactly alike; only their colors distinguish them.

Many flags of the West Indies adapted the Pan-African model by displaying red, black, and green. These colors have come to represent the African-American people—all stemming from the influence of Marcus Garvey, a Jamaican activist who introduced the Pan-African colors to the area. Jamaica, Grenada, Dominica, and St. Kitts all belong to this fairly recent Pan-African color heritage.

Scandinavian flags also have much in common. The cross that appears off-center in most of the region's flags represents a tie to Denmark, which was the first country in the region to adopt a flag. The Danish flag is rooted in Christianity. A legend says that the flag fell from the sky in 1219 and helped King Valdemar II to lead his knights to victory. Finland, Iceland, Norway, and the Faroe Islands all display the off-center cross.

The study of vexillology is really a study of world history. Often flags and their history can tell more in a single symbol than history books can tell in several volumes. Next time you look at a flag of the world or your own state, study it more carefully and try to guess what history might lurk beneath those colors and symbols.

Main Idea and Details *(continued)*

Old Glory Revels in the Stars and Stripes

Its nickname is "Old Glory." Its look has changed countless times. According to some—but not all—historians, the first one was made by Betsy Ross in Philadelphia in 1776. It is the United States flag, whose history is as rich as the nation's.

The story has it that Betsy Ross reveled in telling of the secret delegation of the Continental Congress that asked her to sew the nation's first flag. The three delegates were George Washington, the head of the Continental Army, Robert Morris, the wealthiest and most influential man in the colonies, and Colonel George Ross, a well-known Philadelphian and the uncle of Betsy's husband.

The men brought a rough design, but it was Betsy Ross who brought her artistry and design to the final creation. She was a seamstress and an upholsterer, and showed the committee her prowess with scissors. The one-snip five-pointed star was a specialty, and it so impressed the committee that they urged her to be the original flag maker. The flag was begun in May 1776 and completed a month later.

But before Betsy Ross' flag was made, a number of others had flown in its place. One was the striped "Rattlesnake Flag" used by the Continental Navy. It showed a snake among its stripes with the motto, "Don't Tread on Me." Another popular flag was the "Liberty Tree"

flag, which showed a single green pine tree and the motto, "An Appeal to Heaven." The most popular flag flown was called the "Grand Union" flag, which included thirteen stripes to represent the thirteen colonies and the Union Jack, which was the flag of Britain. With independence just around the corner, the Colonies clearly needed their own flag to represent their new hopeful status. On June 14, 1777, the Continental Congress adopted Betsy Ross' design as the nation's flag.

But variations in the flag's design continued to occur until 1818, when the Flag Act was passed. This finalized the thirteen stripes design and gave the president the power to change the star design, according to the number of states adopted. After that, the flag went through 24 changes, all to add stars, or states, to the flag's field.

Celebrations of the flag happen all the time—on most major holidays, including Memorial Day, Veterans' Day, and of course July 4, Independence Day. But the flag has its own birthday, too—Flag Day, proclaimed June 14. This represents the first day the Continental Congress adopted Betsy Ross' flag. Flag Day celebrations are said to have originated in 1885 when a teacher in Wisconsin arranged for his pupils to observe June 14 as the official day.

Main Idea and Details *(continued)*

Prewriting

Look back at the topics on page 115. Choose the topic that most interests you and that you feel you can write most comfortably about.

Brainstorm

Begin your written answer by brainstorming. Use the web below to help you think of ideas for your topic.

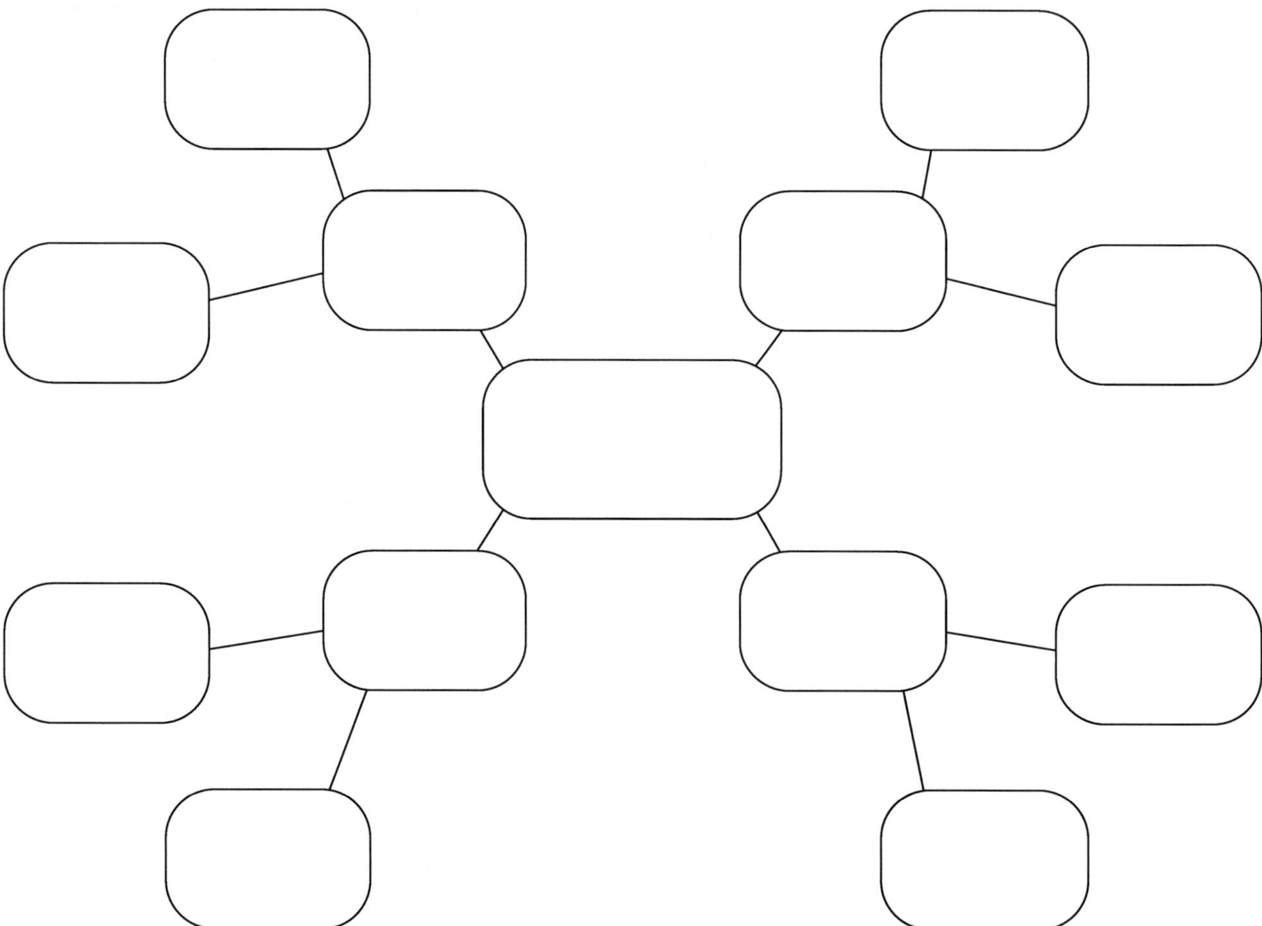

Narrow Your Topic

Now that you have brainstormed the topic, narrrow it down. Remember to ask yourself three questions to help you narrow your topic:

- What part of the topic interests me the most? (What part of my web is most filled in?)
- What part do I know the most about?
- What further information do I need to write my essay?

Write your narrowed topic. ____

Main Idea and Details *(continued)*

Define Your Purpose

It's time to clarify your purpose for writing. Are you writing to inform or explain? Are you writing to describe or analyze? Or are you writing to persuade or express your own opinion or thoughts? Remember to look for the words *explain, describe, analyze, what do you think* in the body of your essay question. Finding these words will often help you define your purpose.

What is your purpose for writing your essay? Write your purpose as a complete sentence that tells what your essay will show.

____

____

Identify Your Audience

Before you begin drafting, think for a moment about your audience—the people who will read your essay. Who is your audience?

____

____

How does this particular audience affect how you will write?

____

____

Main Idea and Details *(continued)*

Drafting

Now it's time to start writing. Remember to highlight the main ideas of what you want to say in the introductory paragraph and use the following paragraphs to develop your supporting ideas. You can use the chart below to help you organize your writing. On a separate sheet of paper, begin the first draft of your essay.

Main Idea

Detail 1

Detail 2

Detail 3

Main Idea and Details *(continued)*

Revising

Remember, the purpose of revising is to step back and look at the big picture of what you are writing about. Refer to your revising checklist to be sure that you have addressed issues of organization, clarity, completeness, and word choice.

Ask youself these questions.

- Do you need to cross anything out?
- Have you created a strong topic sentence?
- Do the paragraphs that follow the introductory paragraph support the main idea?
- Do you need to add any further information?
- Have you written a convincing essay?

Peer Editing

Take time now to revise your essay about flags. You may want to ask a peer to be a sounding board for your essay. Write your second draft using the revisions you have chosen. Be sure to check for transition words, and make sure your conclusion refers to the main idea.

Proofreading

The last thing you need to do is to check your second draft for minor errors, like spelling, grammar, and punctuation. Use your proofreading checklist to be sure that you have covered all the details of your work. Once you've created your final draft, your essay will be ready to share.

Publishing

Write the final draft of your essay following your teacher's guidelines. Be sure that the final draft is free of mistakes and is clear, clean, and easy to read. Create a title that captures the interest of the reader.

Lesson 9
Cause and Effect

Have you ever taken a test or a quiz you didn't study for? What happened? Chances are you didn't do too well (unless you were very lucky!). Have you ever forgotten to wear a jacket outside in 20-degree weather? What happened? Probably you were very cold. Have you ever eaten too much at a meal? What happened? No doubt you felt sick or thoroughly stuffed.

The three examples above all describe events and the reasons they happen. **If** you don't wear a jacket, **then** you get cold. **If** you don't study, **then** you do poorly. This kind of connection between events is called **cause and effect.** The **effect** is the thing that happens. The **cause** is the reason the thing happens. **If** you eat too much (cause), **then** you will feel stuffed (effect).

Cause		Effect
don't wear a jacket	⟶	get cold
don't study	⟶	do poorly on test
eat too much	⟶	feel stuffed

You use cause-and-effect writing when you want to tell reasons for things happening, explanations for events that take place, or answers to why people behave a certain way. It is most often used when writing to explain, inform, or analyze why something happened, how something happened, or what made something happen.

In real life, causes necessarily come before their effects. In writing, however, this is not always the case. The effects may be described first, and the causes may be explained afterwards. Let's reword an example from above to show how this reversal works: You got cold because you did not wear a jacket. In sequence, the leaving behind the jacket happened first, but it is listed second in the sentence.

Causes and effects do not always appear in the same sentence. Sometimes descriptions, details, and explanations come between them. The relationship between the cause and the effect should always be clear, however—that is the point of cause-and-effect writing.

Cause and Effect *(continued)*

Model

Read the paragraph below and see if you can identify the cause-and-effect relationships.

Fire in the Shop

On March 25, 1911, at 4:30 P.M., over 500 immigrant Jewish women were finishing their shift as garment makers at the Triangle Shirtwaist factory in New York City. They were tired and ready to go home because their managers worked them very hard without giving breaks or time to stretch during the long shifts. The managers even locked the exit doors to keep the women from leaving early. On this day, one of the workers noticed a small fire in a rag bin on the eighth floor. Within 15 minutes, the fire had spread throughout the eighth floor and 146 women who were trapped in the building were killed. This event was horrible: It was the worst fire in the history of New York City up to that point. But the event also changed the course of working history. The owners were charged with manslaughter. Labor unions organized to demand safer working conditions for their workers. As a result of the fire, working conditions all over the United States improved, and workers' safety became an essential part of the workday world.

Some words give you a clue that there is a cause-and-effect relationship. One clue word is *because*. In the second sentence of "Fire in the Shop," *because* signals such a relationship. In this case, the effect comes first: "They were tired and ready to go home." The cause for this follows: "because their managers worked them very hard without giving breaks or time to stretch during the long shifts."

Another clue appears in the last sentence. "As a result" signals a cause-and-effect relationship. In that sentence, "the fire" is the cause, and "working conditions improved and workers' safety became an essential part of the workday world" are the effects.

Sometimes, the cause-and-effect relationship is not signaled with a particular word or phrase. The article states that 146 women were trapped in the burning factory. Earlier, the reader learns that "managers even locked the exit doors." Although the article does not state that all the women died because the exits were locked, the reader concludes that this was a contributing cause.

Cause and Effect *(continued)*

Try It

Read the following article about Rosa Parks and the Civil Rights movement. Identify the cause-and-effect relationships.

Boycotting for Seats

Rosa Parks reluctantly accepted the honor of being called "The Mother of the Civil Rights Movement." She was quick to say that she did not create the movement by herself. But her actions on December 1, 1955, began a chain of events that changed the course of history.

On this December day, Rosa Parks, a department store seamstress, boarded the bus as she always did in the early evening. She passed by the mostly empty "whites-only" seats and sat in the middle of the bus. She was allowed to sit there, as long as there weren't any white people who wanted a seat. As the bus continued along its route, more and more white people climbed aboard. Soon the "whites-only" section was full. When the bus driver noticed that one white man was standing, he ordered the African Americans sitting in Parks' row to move back. According to Parks, "The other three all stood up. But the driver saw me still sitting there. He said would I stand up, and I said, 'No, I will not.' Then he said, 'I'll have you arrested.' And I told him he could do that. So he didn't

move the bus any further. Several black people left the bus."

"I didn't have any idea what my actions would bring about," Rosa Parks said. But the bus driver brought charges against her and as a result, four days later, the Montgomery Bus Boycott began. This boycott was organized by Dr. Martin Luther King, Jr. It lasted 381 days—a little over a year. During that time, African Americans in Montgomery found other ways to go to and from work.

It was hard to keep up the boycott. But it paid off in the end. Because of the chain of events begun by Rosa Parks' bus ride home from work, on November 13, 1956, the Supreme Court declared that Alabama's segregation laws were not valid. Montgomery tried not to obey the new law, but on December 20, 1956, the bus company officials were forced to open the buses to everyone. The bus boycott was the beginning of an entire movement, which resulted in several laws changing and a whole society accepting African Americans as people deserving equal rights.

Can you identify at least two cause-and-effect relationships in this article?

1. ____

   ____

2. ____

   ____

Cause and Effect *(continued)*

Good Writing Tip: Use Cause-and-Effect Words

When you write using a cause-and-effect pattern, remember that you are writing to show *why, how, what caused, how did,* or *what made* something happen. Writing in this pattern is very common when you are writing about social studies or history. It helps you discover why things happened and what the results were in the course of history.

When you are writing in a cause-and-effect pattern, you can often use words that signal that you are explaining why or how something took place. Here are lists of words you might use to describe cause and effect.

Cause		Effect	
because	if . . .	as a result	therefore
due to	began	consequently	leads to (led to)
since		thus	so
as a result of		resulted in	. . . then

Look at the article about Rosa Parks on page 124. Underline any words you see that demonstrate a cause-and-effect relationship. Write those words below and tell whether they are describing the cause or the effect.

Cause-and-effect words: ____

____

Application

Now it's your turn to try your hand at organizing an essay using the cause-and-effect pattern. Below is a list of possible writing topics. All of them are related to the articles that follow on two inventions that changed the world. Select the topic that most interests you. Then follow the steps in the writing process to make your essay the best it can be.

1. It has been said that the invention of the printing press completely revolutionized society. In what ways do you think the press might have changed the world?

2. How would your life be different if the car had never been invented? Think not only of your own life, but life generations ago. Would you live where you live today?

3. Which invention, the car or the printing press, do you think had the most significant impact on society? Give reasons for your answer.

Cause and Effect *(continued)*

Creating the First Editions

Unemployment may have been high in 1450, but not if you were a scribe. In 1450, there were no computers, no typewriters, no stencils, no press-on type. If you wanted to write something, you called on a scribe, who brought out sheepskin vellum and a feather and expensive ink. Then the feather was dipped in the expensive ink, words were *scribed*, or written, and the feather dipped again and again and again. In 1450, virtually everyone who could write worked as a scribe in a *scriptorium*, or writing shop.

Also employed in 1450 was Johannes Gutenberg, a German goldsmith and businessman. He knew from his business life that tasks like keeping books, creating receipts, bills, and documents were becoming more and more of a necessity. But it was becoming harder and harder for scribes to keep up with his demands and those of the numerous new businesses that were springing up.

In the meantime, the Catholic Church, which was the economic, social, and cultural center of society, needed more and more scribes to conduct its business.

And so Gutenberg, like all good entrepreneurs, saw an opportunity. What would happen, he thought, if a machine were created that could produce cheap—and quick—writing? He brought together the technologies of machines that already existed— textile presses, papermaking machines, and wine presses. He combined those machines with a way of molding and casting a steel "punch" or chunk of metal. Into each of these punches was carved a letter, which was then used as a type letter. The width of the letter bases varied. For example, the *i* was very narrow and the *m* was very wide, causing a variety of letter sizes. This variety in letters in turn gave a rhythm to the printed word, which looked sophisticated, elegant, and easy to read.

Gutenberg's first printed work was a Bible written in Latin. His first run of his now-famous "Gutenberg Bible" was 300 two-volume copies. These books sold for the equivalent of a scribe's earnings for three years. And they had taken very little time to produce. Soon the church saw real potential for Gutenberg's type machine. They could create more bibles, more books on Christianity, doctrine and policy statements, and send them all over Europe—and beyond.

But the church and businesses weren't the only ones who saw the benefits of Gutenberg's invention. Those who were disagreeing with the church's stand on many social and spiritual issues took advantage of the new writing method as well. One man in particular—Martin Luther— found the printed word a way to spread his ideas throughout Europe, which eventually led to a reform movement of the Catholic Church.

(continued)

Cause and Effect *(continued)*

Creating the First Editions (continued)

In 1476, an Englishman named William Caxton set up the first printing press in England. His mission was to increase the number of people reading popular literature. He was an editor and a translator who saw Gutenberg's invention as a great way to get people reading. The problem was that in England, there were so many different dialects and variations in the language that there was no one standard usage. Caxton changed that by printing—and editing—books and standardizing the spelling, diction, and usage for all the books he printed.

Gutenberg and Caxton's first presses were run by hand. Clerks would move the type around and then press the words onto a sheet of paper. In 1884, over 400 years after Gutenberg's invention, the Linotype machine was created. This allowed the type to be moved by machine rather than by hand. This invention speeded up the printing process even more.

Innovations continue to be made in the printing world. Word processing machines; computers; dot matrix, inkjet, and laser printers all serve to make print faster and easier. The result is that information is relayed faster and more efficiently throughout the world. Today there are no longer scriptoria. But there are cyber-cafes, copy shops, printers, and publishers to keep all our present-day scribes busy and profitable.

Cause and Effect *(continued)*

Running the Roads of History

The car was invented in 1335. Yes, that's 1335, not a typo! In this year, before the printing press was even invented, several Italian designers created the prototype for a wind-driven vehicle with wheels and gears. But while they designed these vehicles, they never were able to build them.

The first "car" to move under its own power was designed by the Frenchman Nicholas Joseph Cugnot and built by M. Brézin in 1769. In 1770, a second car was built expressly to haul cannons around Paris. On its first voyage, this car chugged up to its fastest speed—two miles an hour—and then hit a stonewall. This was perhaps a better ending than if it had tipped over, which the new models had a tendency to do, unless they were already weighted with a cannon in the back. These early models weighed 4 tons, or 8,000 pounds.

After these models were tried and not quite perfected, inventors set their sights on creating a car that ran on iron rails, which led to the birth of the railway car. But the idea for the self-powered vehicle nagged inventors through the next century. Several inventors contributed to the invention of what is now the modern automobile. They all faced the same huge challenge: how to power the vehicle. Some inventors tried gunpowder to blast the cars into movement. Others experimented with coal gas, which helped, but didn't catapult the invention into the hands of the public. Various engineers and scientists like Nikolaus Otto, Gottlieb Daimler, and Karl Benz

worked at perfecting a combustion engine that would run on gas. In the last years of the nineteenth century, would-be inventors were tinkering with trials and failures of creating an automobile that would run on steam.

In 1893, the Duryea brothers, twins Charles and Frank, issued the first gas-powered car in the United States. Its test run was September 21, 1893, in Springfield, Massachusetts. The car was manufactured out of a buggy carriage and a single-cylinder gas engine. The car didn't run too well, however, and Frank put it away in storage until many years later. However, the Duryeas are considered the pioneers of the automobile industry.

In the meantime, Henry Ford, of Detroit, Michigan, was also working on a gas-powered car. His first car was built in 1896, and sold for $200. He quickly put the money from the first into building a second car. But the car "bug" still hadn't caught on, and Ford didn't sell another car until 1903.

Ford's strengths lay not as an inventor, but as an innovator. He scoured the work of efficiency expert Frederick W. Taylor for ideas about how to manage and create better efficiency. Taylor's book was a catalyst for Ford because it jogged him into thinking about ways he could produce more cars for more people—by being more efficient. Borrowing from existing technology, he created the moving assembly line. This meant that several people could work on a car at once, rather than

(continued)

Cause and Effect *(continued)*

Running the Roads of History (continued)

just one person crafting the entire car. The car would move slowly along the line, and each worker would contribute one piece to the car. This way, thousands of cars could be manufactured quickly and thus sold for less money. This made the car accessible to all kinds of people, not just those who were wealthy.

The first of Henry Ford's cars cost $950 in 1908. But because of the efficiency of the moving assembly line, the price was soon reduced to under $300. By 1914, Ford's Motor Company was turning out a car at a rate of 1 every 24 seconds! Henry Ford got very rich, clearing roughly $25,000 profit a day. He raised the wages of his workers to $5.00 an hour, an unprecedented wage for the time. This was one way that he could keep them doing the very monotonous work along the assembly line and entice them to put up with his strict and tyrannical leadership style.

By 1916, Congress enacted highway fund legislation and the United States began an era of road building. For the first time, people could travel wherever they wanted to, whenever they wanted to. People began to move from the inner cities to the suburbs because they could commute easily into the city and go home at night to a more beautiful place. Hotels, motels, and roadside restaurants sprang up. Even families that had once clustered in towns began to move apart, paying visits by automobile. The consequences of the invention of the car are far-reaching, including our present-day challenge of how to deal with the pollution it causes.

Every year, the car evolves and changes. New safety and design features come out with every model. The evolution of the automobile is by no means over!

Cause and Effect *(continued)*

Prewriting

Choose the topic on page 125 that most interests you and that you feel you can write most comfortably about.

Brainstorm

Use the web below to help you brainstorm about your topic.

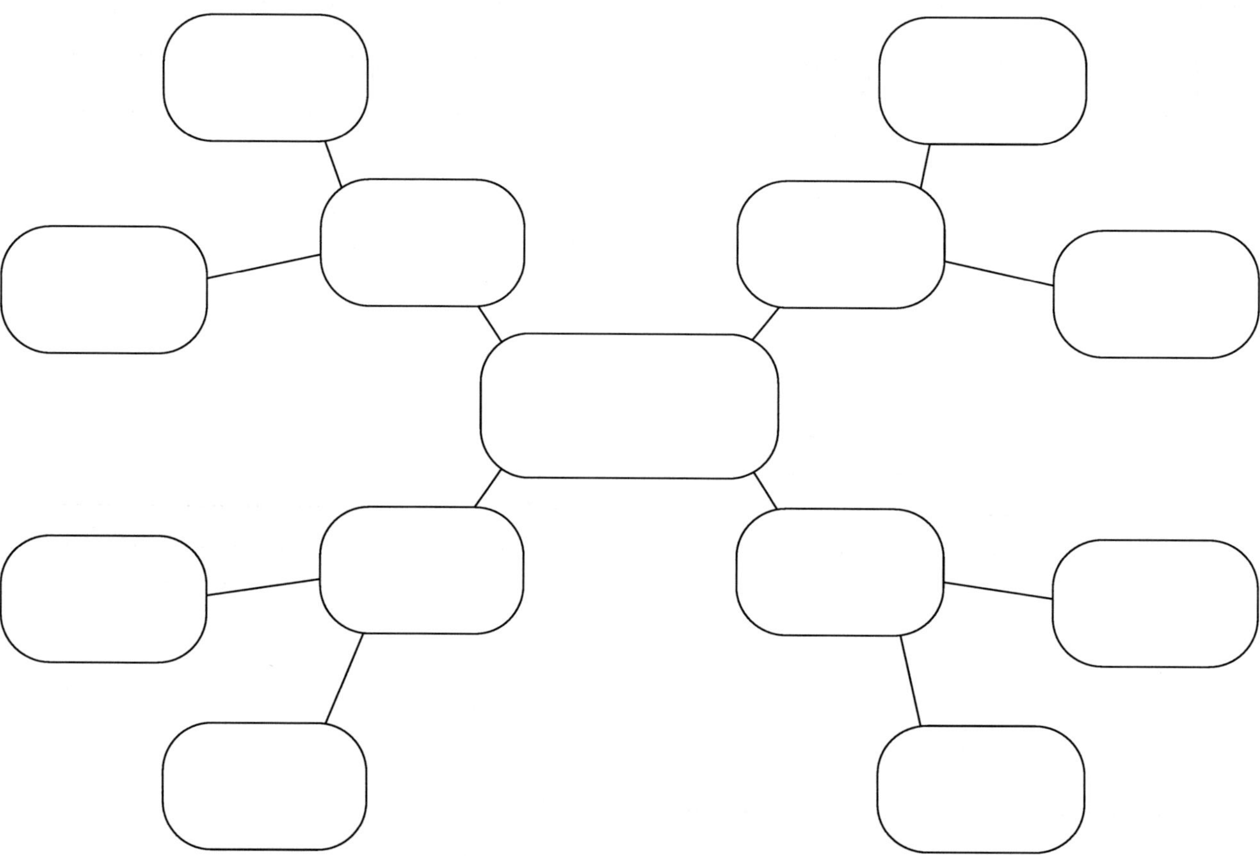

Narrow Your Topic

Analyze your brainstorming web. Write your narrowed topic.

Define Your Purpose

Write one complete sentence that tells what your essay will show.

Identify Your Audience

Who will read your essay? How does this affect your writing?

Cause and Effect *(continued)*

Drafting

Now it's time to start writing. As you remember, this is a time to practice writing in the pattern that shows cause-and-effect relationships. You can use one of the charts below to help you organize your writing.

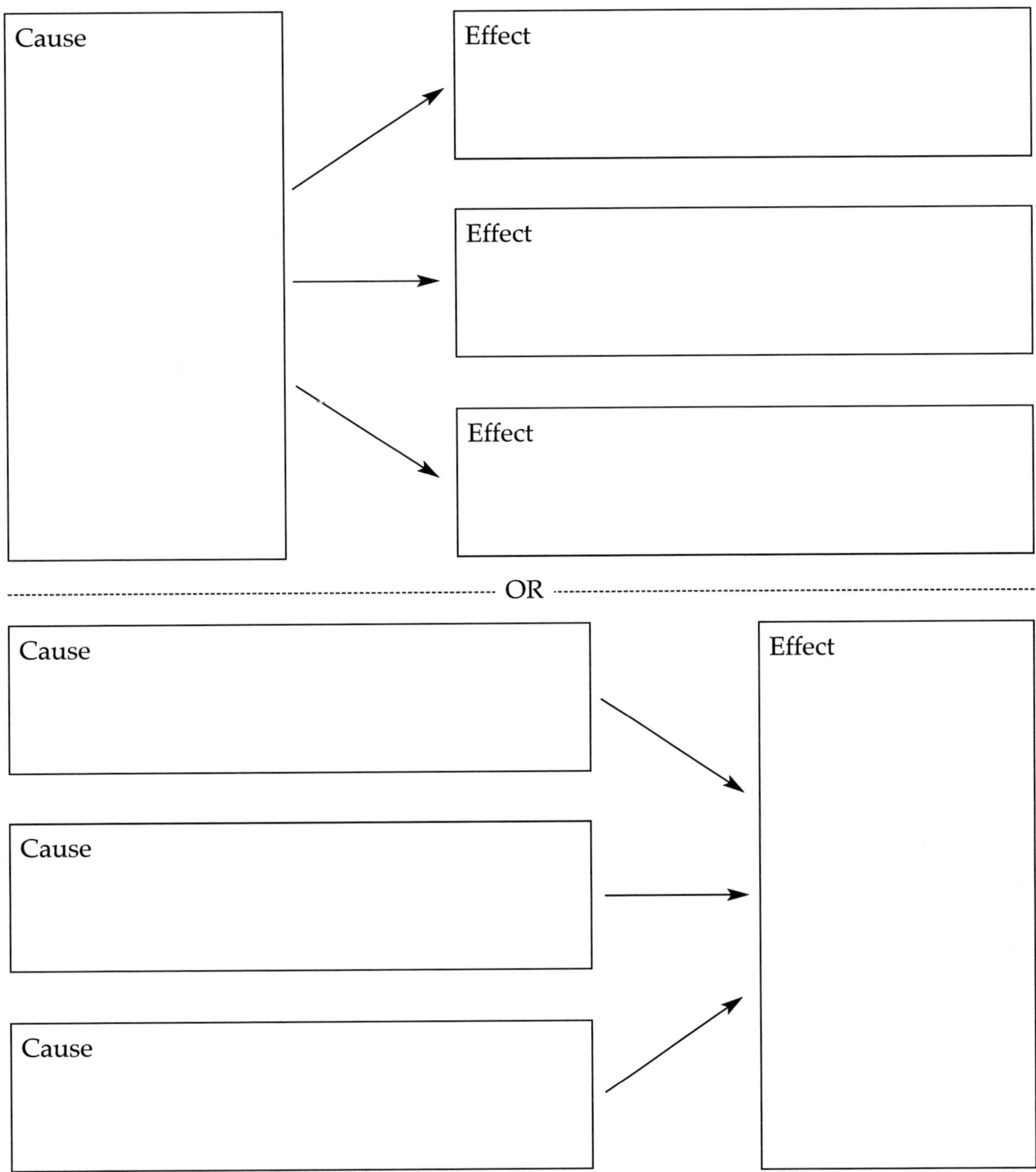

On a separate sheet of paper, begin the first draft of your essay on the topic you chose.

Cause and Effect *(continued)*

Revising

Remember, the first part of revising is to step back and look at the big picture of what you are writing about.

Ask yourself these questions.

- Do you need to cross anything out?

- Is your purpose clear in the first paragraph?

- Are your cause-and-effect relationships clear?

- Have you used cause-and-effect words to mark transitions and indicate events and reasons?

Peer Editing

You may also want to call on a peer to be a sounding board for your essay. Write your second draft using the revising checklist.

Proofreading

The last thing you need to do is to check your work for minor errors, like spelling, grammar, and punctuation. Use your proofreading checklist from your teacher to be sure that you have covered all the details in your second draft.

Publishing

Write the final draft of your essay following your teacher's guidelines. Be sure that the final draft is free of mistakes and is clear, clean, and easy to read. Create an interesting title.

<u>Lesson 10</u>
Compare and Contrast

You've learned so far about three important organizational patterns in writing: chronological order, main idea and details, and cause and effect. The next organizational pattern that you'll learn is called **compare and contrast.** When you compare and contrast things—ideas, events, individuals or characters, or behaviors— you are showing the ways that they are similar (compare) and the ways that they are different (contrast).

Compare

The compare-and-contrast pattern is used when you are describing things. It can also be used when you are defining things, when you are making an argument, or when you are analyzing things. This pattern is very flexible—you can use it almost any time you write!

A good comparison essay will show

- how two things that appear similar are actually different (a llama and an alpaca)
- how two things that appear to be different are actually similar (soccer and English football)

Contrast

When you write in a compare-and-contrast pattern, you often compare first the most striking or important parts of the events, persons, or ideas you are discussing. For example, if you were to talk about McIntosh apples and Gala apples, you would begin by naming their obvious similarities: they are both apples. Then you can break down your comparison by doing one of these things:

- Show how the things you are comparing are alike, then show how they are different.
- Examine one idea thoroughly, then examine the other.

Compare and Contrast *(continued)*

Model

Read the following compare-and-contrast article.

Ship (or is it boat?) Watch

"In fourteen hundred and ninety-two, Columbus sailed the ocean blue." Few would dispute the truth to this age-old rhyme, but many might dispute the tricky question: Did Columbus sail a ship or a boat—and what's the difference between them?

After all, ships and boats have much in common. They both float atop the water. They both have relatively flat bottoms, they are waterproof (one hopes!), and they carry passengers or cargo. Ships and boats can be used to travel distances, they can both sink, and they are both steered with a wheel and a rudder. Sailboats and sailing ships both use wind to propel them, and motorboats and motorized ships use an engine to propel them.

These two vehicles have differences, too. For example, a sailing ship is a square-rigged vessel with at least three masts. A sailboat also sails, but it has fewer than three masts. A motorized ship is big and is used to cross oceans and travel in very deep water. A motorboat is not big and isn't used to cross oceans or travel in deep water. One good rule of thumb to remember the difference is to note that a ship is big enough to carry a boat; on the other hand, a boat is small enough to be carried on a ship!

In this article, the two things—ships and boats—are first compared, then contrasted. The reading begins with similarities, then moves to differences.

Good Writing Tip: Use Compare and Contrast Words

You can write a compare-and-contrast essay by using key words. One of the best ways to show comparison or contrast is to use comparative language with the *-er* or *-est* suffixes. Other words, like those below, can be used when writing in the compare and contrast pattern.

Compare Words		Contrast Words	
additionally	in the same way	although	opposite
alike	like	but	or
also	likewise	conversely	still
both	similarly	different from	unlike
common	too	in contrast	whereas
further		in spite of	yet
in addition		on the other hand	

Compare and Contrast *(continued)*

Go back to the article, "Ship (or is it boat?) Watch." List the compare words and the contrast words the author used.

Compare Words	Contrast Words

Try It

Look at the short article below about Guam and Puerto Rico. As you read, note what is being compared and what is being contrasted. Identify the compare-and-contrast signal words.

The Two Tiny Territories

When is a state not a state? When it's a territory. That's the answer you'll find when you're looking for information about the United States' two island territories—Guam and Puerto Rico.

These islands have much in common. Both were ceded to the United States by Spain after the Spanish-American War in 1898. Both islands' residents are citizens of the United States. Both islands call the president of the United States their chief of state. Both islands enjoy a tropical marine climate. In addition, tourism is a major part of both of their economies. Guam and Puerto Rico both use the U.S. dollar for their currency. And further, they are both relatively small in size. Guam is roughly three times the size of Washington, D.C. Puerto Rico is larger, just under three times the size of Rhode Island.

But these island territories are very different, too. Guam has a population of 157,557 people (July 2001). Puerto Rico has nearly 25 times Guam's population at 3,937,316 (July 2001). Most of Guam's land is made up of volcanic rock, whereas Puerto Rico's land is mostly mountainous. The principal language in Guam is English, whereas in Puerto Rico, it is Spanish.

Guam's economy is based on military dollars spent at the large military bases there. Guam also exports fish and handicrafts. Puerto Rico, on the other hand, has a very diverse economy. Industry leads the way, followed by agriculture and tourism. Over five million tourists visit Puerto Rico annually.

Both islands are great places to visit. Both sport lovely beaches and a warm, comfortable climate. And both are part of the United States—so you don't even need a passport to visit!

Look through the article above on Guam and Puerto Rico and underline the compare-and-contrast words.

Compare and Contrast *(continued)*

Venn Diagram

One great way to illustrate the ways that two things are alike or different is to use a graphic organizer called a Venn diagram. A Venn diagram is very simple. It consists of two intersecting circles, like this:

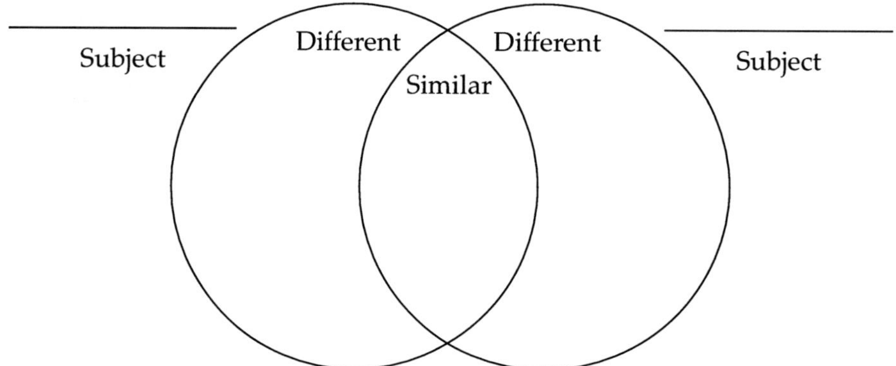

When you are comparing and contrasting two things, you can use a Venn diagram to quickly note the similarities and differences between them. At the top of the first circle, write the first thing that is being compared. At the top of the second circle, write the second thing that is being compared. Then list all the similarities between the two things in the part of the circles that intersects. List all the qualities that are unique to each thing outside the intersecting circles.

You can also use a Venn diagram to compare more than two things. Just add another circle, but be sure that all three circles intersect!

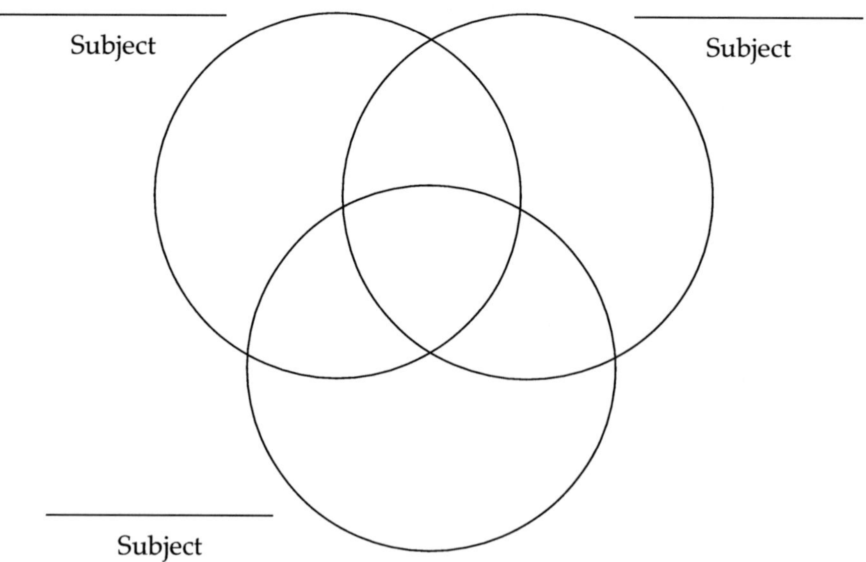

Compare and Contrast *(continued)*

Look at the Venn diagram below. List all the things that are alike about Guam and Puerto Rico in the center of the diagram. Then list all the things that are different, or unique, in the circles outside the intersection.

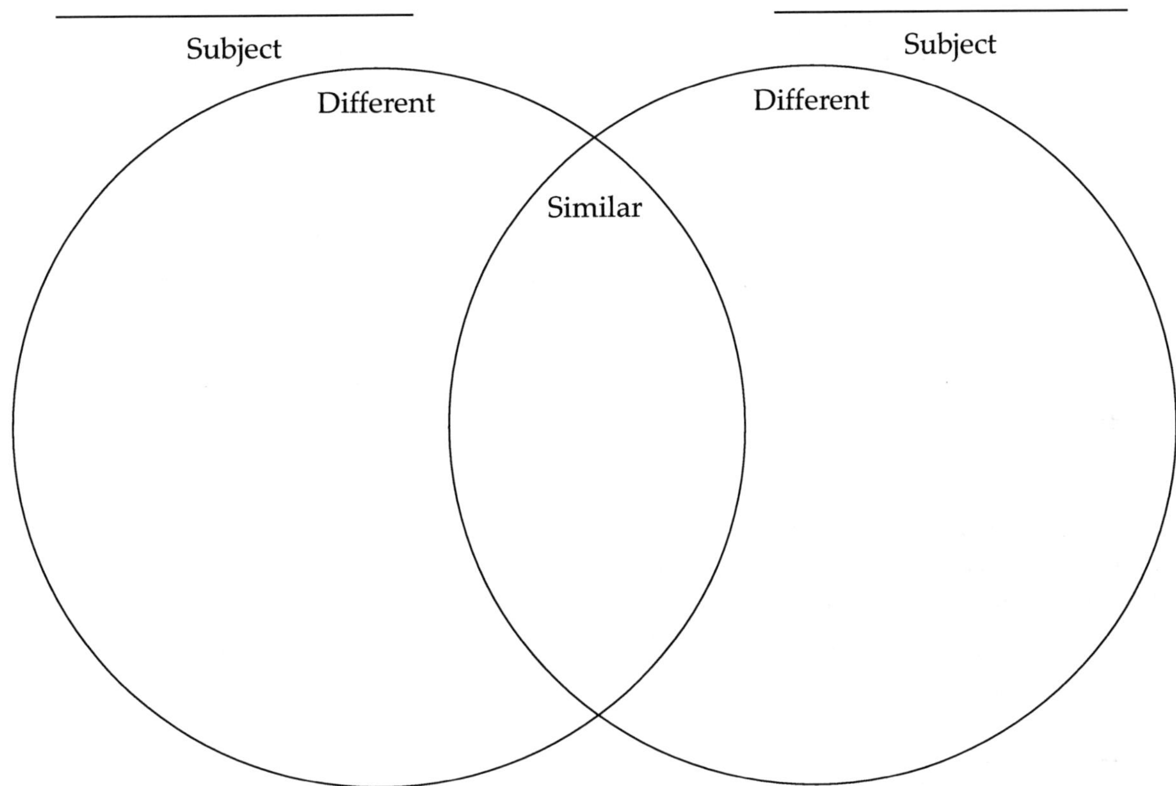

Compare and Contrast *(continued)*

Application

Now it's your turn to try your hand at organizing an essay using the compare-and-contrast pattern. Below is a list of possible writing topics. All of them are related to the articles that follow about fashion reform. Select the topic that most interests you. Then follow the steps in the writing process and use the compare-and-contrast pattern to write your essay.

1. In what ways are Mark Twain and Elizabeth Cady Stanton's ideas on dress reform alike? In what ways are they different? Give examples to support your answer.

2. Do you agree or disagree with Elizabeth Cady Stanton's ideas on dress reform? Why?

3. If you were writing an excerpt in your autobiography about dress reform, what would you say? How would your comments be like those of Mark Twain or Elizabeth Cady Stanton?

The Man in the White Flannel Suit

In December 1906, the colorful writer Mark Twain was asked to address Congress about his feelings about copyright laws. Before he made his address, he was socializing with various news reporters who had come to Washington to cover the Congressional session. As was his custom, Mark Twain (aka Samuel Clemens) took the opportunity to speak to the reporters about something he felt strongly about: dress reform. Here is an excerpt from an article in The New York Times *the day after his visit to Congress.*

from The New York Times, *December 8, 1906*

Advocates . . . Dress Reform. Mark Twain in White Amuses Congressmen. Wears Light Flannel Suit. Says at 71 Dark Colors Depress Him . . .

WASHINGTON, Dec. 7—Mark Twain spent a busy afternoon at the Capitol today, and for half an hour entertained the newspaper correspondents with a characteristic talk. Despite the blustering wind which swept down Pennsylvania Avenue, the author wore a suit of white flannels. In the members' gallery, which he first visited to watch the proceedings of the House, he attracted general attention . . .

(continued)

Compare and Contrast *(continued)*

An Advocate of Dress Reform (continued)

While waiting to appear before the committee Mr. Clemens talked to the reporters.

"Why don't you ask why I am wearing such apparently unseasonable clothes? I'll tell you. I have found that when a man reaches the advanced age of 71 years as I have, the continual sight of dark clothing is likely to have a depressing effect upon him. Light-colored clothing is more pleasing to the eye and enlivens the spirit. Now, of course, I cannot compel everyone to wear such clothing just for my especial benefit, so I do the next best thing and wear it myself.

"Of course, before a man reaches my years, the fear of criticism might prevent him from indulging his fancy. I am not afraid of that. I am decidedly for pleasing color combinations in dress. I like to see the women's clothes, say, at the opera. What can be more depressing than the sombre black which custom requires men to wear upon state occasions. A group of men in evening clothes looks like a flock of crows, and is just about as inspiring.

"After all, what is the purpose of clothing? Are not clothes intended primarily to preserve dignity and also to afford comfort to their wearer? Now I know of nothing more uncomfortable than the present day clothes of men. The finest clothing made is a person's own skin but, of course, society demands something more than this.

"The best-dressed man I have ever seen, however, was a native of the Sandwich Islands, who attracted my attention thirty years ago. Now, when that man wanted to don especial dress to honor a public occasion or a holiday, why he occasionally put on a pair of spectacles. Otherwise the clothing with which God had provided him sufficed.

"Of course, I have ideas of dress reform. For one thing, why not adopt some of the women's styles? Goodness knows, they adopt enough of ours. Take the peek-a-boo waist, for instance. It has the obvious advantages of being cool and comfortable, and in addition it is almost always made up in pleasing colors, which cheer and do not depress.

"It is true that I dressed the Connecticut Yankee at King Arthur's Court in a plug hat, but let's see, that was twenty-five years ago. Then no man was considered fully dressed until he donned a plug hat. Nowadays I think that no man is dressed until he leaves it home. Why, when I left home yesterday they trotted out a plug hat for me to wear.

" 'You must wear it,' they told me: 'why, just think of going to Washington without a plug hat!' But I said no; I would wear a derby or nothing. Why, I believe I could walk along the streets of New York—I never do—but still I think I could— and I should never see a well-dressed man wearing a plug hat. If I did I should suspect him of something. I don't know just what, but I would suspect him.

(continued)

Compare and Contrast *(continued)*

An Advocate of Dress Reform (continued)

"Why, when I got up on the second story of that Pennsylvania ferryboat coming down here yesterday, I saw Howells [a colleague of Twain's] coming along. He was the only man on the boat with a plug hat, and I tell you he felt ashamed of himself. He said he had been persuaded to wear it against his better sense, but just think of a man nearly 70 years old who has not a mind of his own on such matters!"

The Woman in Bloomers

The following is an excerpt from the autobiography of Elizabeth Cady Stanton, one of the first women's rights activists. She refers to Seneca Falls, New York, which was the home of the women's movement as it was the site of the first women's rights conference.

The Bloomer Dress

There was one bright woman among the many in our Seneca Falls literary circle to whom I would give more than a passing notice—Mrs. Amelia Bloomer, who represented three novel phases of woman's life. She was assistant postmistress; an editor of a reform paper [the *Lily*] advocating temperance and woman's rights; and an advocate of the new costume which bore her name!

. . . Although she wore the bloomer dress, its originator was Elizabeth Smith Miller [Stanton's cousin], the only daughter of Gerrit Smith [the abolitionist]. In the winter of 1852 Mrs. Miller came to visit me in Seneca Falls, dressed somewhat in the Turkish style—short skirt, full trousers of fine black broadcloth; a Spanish cloak, of the same material, reaching to the knee; beaver hat and feathers and dark furs; altogether a most becoming costume and exceedingly convenient for walking in all kinds of weather. To see my cousin, with a lamp in one hand and a baby in the other, walk upstairs with ease and grace, while, with flowing robes, I pulled myself up with difficulty, lamp and baby out of the question, readily convinced me that there was sore need of reform in woman's dress, and I promptly donned a similar attire. What incredible freedom I enjoyed for two years! Like a captive set free from his ball and chain, I was always ready for a brisk walk through sleet and snow and rain, to climb a mountain, jump over a fence, work in the garden, and, in fact, for any necessary locomotion.

. . . Mrs. Bloomer having the *Lily* in which to discuss the merits of the new dress, the press generally took up the question, and much valuable information was elicited on the physiological results of woman's fashionable attire; the crippling effect of tight waists and long skirts, the heavy weight on the hips, and high heels, all combined to throw the

(continued)

Compare and Contrast *(continued)*

The Bloomer Dress (continued)

spine out of plumb and lay the foundation for all manner of nervous diseases. But while all agreed that some change was absolutely necessary for the health of women, the press stoutly ridiculed those who were ready to make the experiment.

A few sensible women, in different parts of the country, adopted the costume, and farmers' wives especially proved its convenience. It was also worn by skaters, gymnasts, tourists, and in sanitariums. But, while the few realized its advantages, the many laughed it to scorn, and heaped such ridicule on its wearers that they soon found that the physical freedom enjoyed did not compensate for the persistent persecution and petty annoyances suffered at every turn. To be rudely gazed at in public and private, to be the conscious subjects of criticism, and to be followed by crowds of boys in the streets, were all, to the very last degree, exasperating. A favorite doggerel that our tormentors

chanted, when we appeared in public places, ran thus:

> Heigh! ho! in rain and snow,
> The bloomer now is all the go.
> Twenty tailors take the stitches,
> Twenty women wear the breeches.
> Heigh! ho! in rain or snow,
> The bloomer now is all the go.

The singers were generally invisible behind some fence or attic window. . . . The patience of most of us was exhausted in about two years; but our leader, Mrs. Miller, bravely adhered to the costume for nearly seven years. . . . She was bravely sustained, however, by her husband, Colonel Miller, who never flinched in escorting his wife and her coadjutors. . . . Mrs. Miller was also encouraged by the intense feeling of her father on the question of women's dress. To him the whole revolution in woman's position turned on her dress. The long skirt was the symbol of her degradation.

Compare and Contrast *(continued)*

Prewriting

Choose a topic from page 138.

Brainstorm

Use the web below to help you brainstorm about your topic.

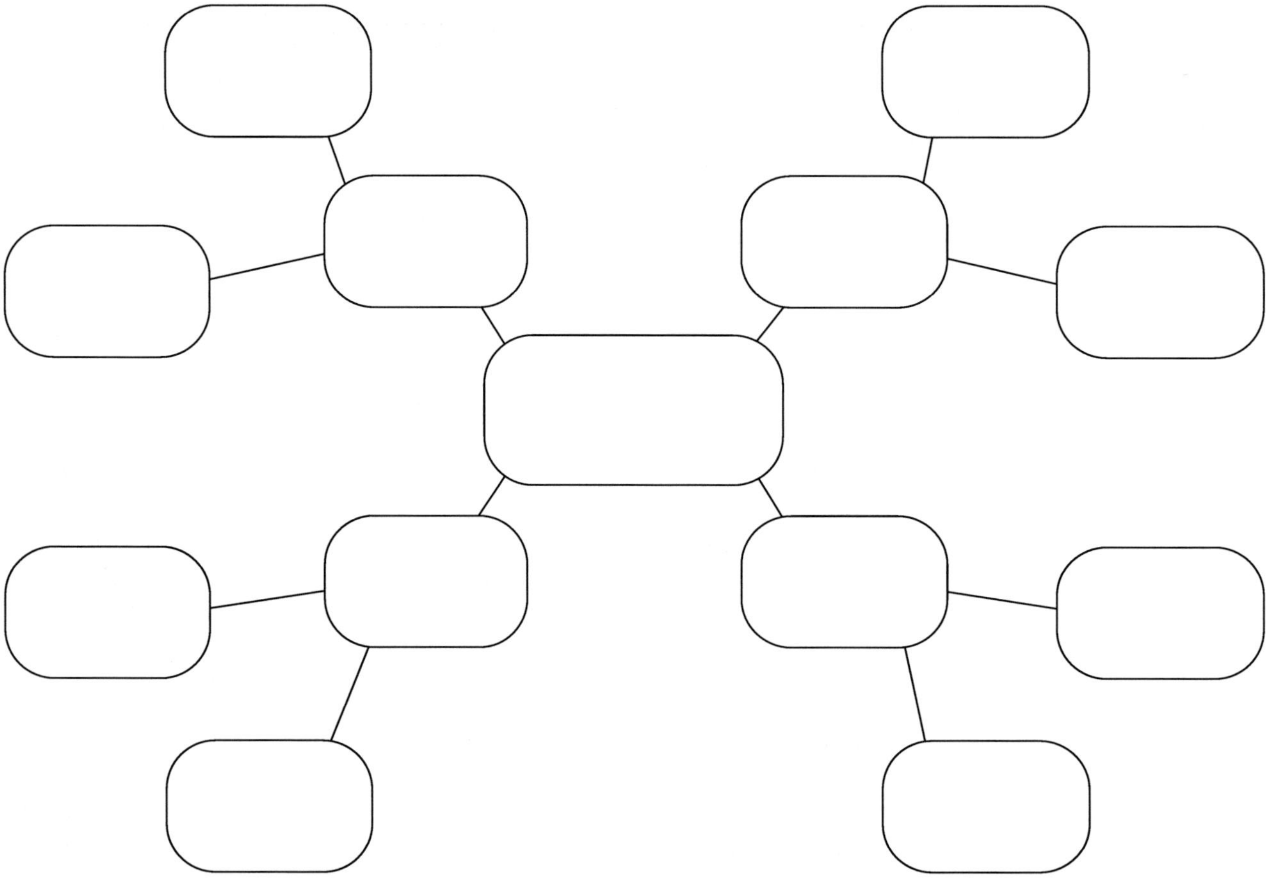

Narrow Your Topic

Analyse your web to narrow your broad topic. Write your narrowed topic.

____

Define Your Purpose

Write one complete sentence that tells your purpose.

____

Identify Your Audience

Who will read your essay? How does your audience affect your writing?

____

Compare and Contrast *(continued)*

Drafting

Now it's time to start writing. Before you do, look at the ideas on your brainstorming web that fit your narrowed topic. Then transfer them to this Venn diagram so you can organize your essay into a compare-and-contrast pattern.

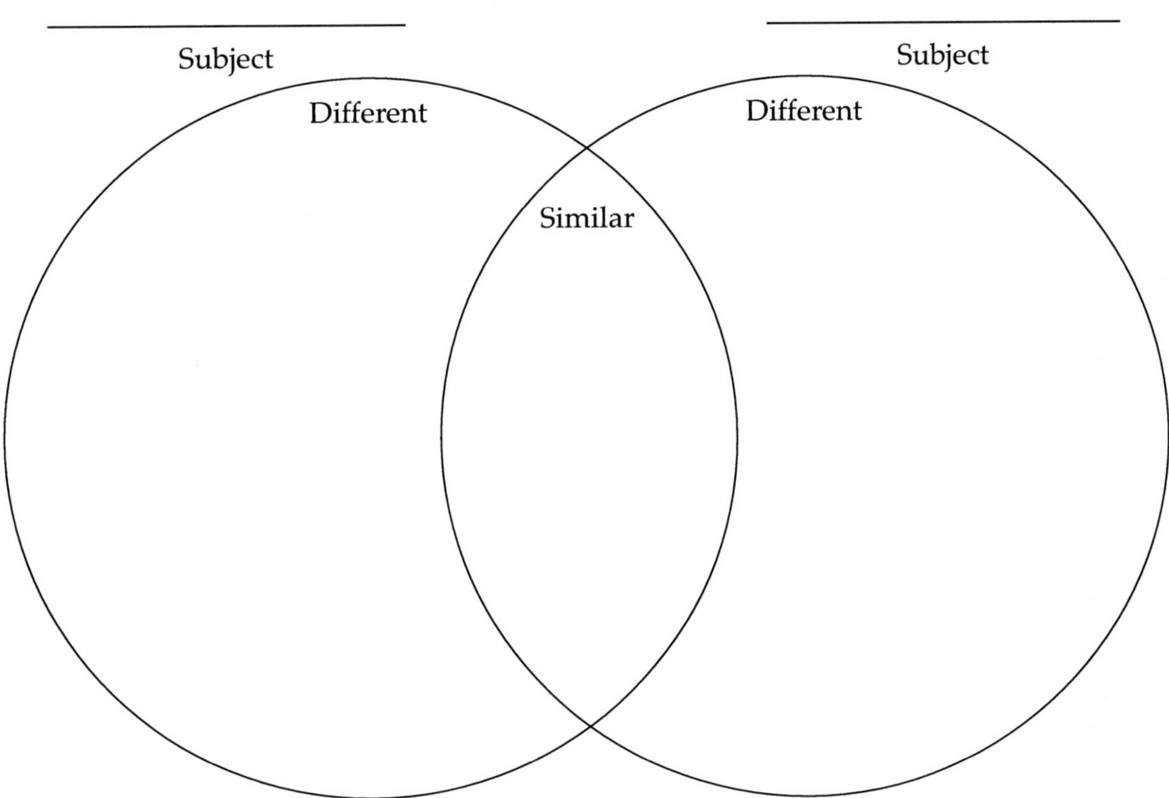

On a separate sheet of paper, begin the first draft of your essay.

Compare and Contrast *(continued)*

Revising

Step back and look at the big picture of what you are writing about. Ask yourself these questions.

- Is what you are comparing and contrasting clear?
- Have you used comparing and contrasting words to mark transitions and show how your subjects are similar and different?
- Is your essay organized?

Peer Editing

Now revise your essay. Use your revising checklist from your teacher and insight from a peer. Write your second draft using the revisions you have chosen. Check for comparing and contrasting signal words. Be sure you don't jump from comparing to contrasting in the same paragraph.

Proofreading

The last thing to do is to check your work for minor errors, like spelling, grammar, and punctuation. Use your proofreading checklist from your teacher for help.

Publishing

Write the final draft of your essay following your teacher's guidelines. Be sure that the final draft is free of mistakes and is clear, clean, and easy to read. Create an interesting title.

Blank Graphic Organizers

The graphic organizers in this section may be copied for students to use in conjunction with their reading and writing assignments.

4-P Chart

1. Preview	2. Predict	3. Prior Knowledge	4. Purpose

KWL Chart

K **What I KNOW**	W **What I WANT to Know**	L **What I LEARNED**

SQ3R Chart

S Survey	Q Question	R Read	R Recall	R Reflect

Web

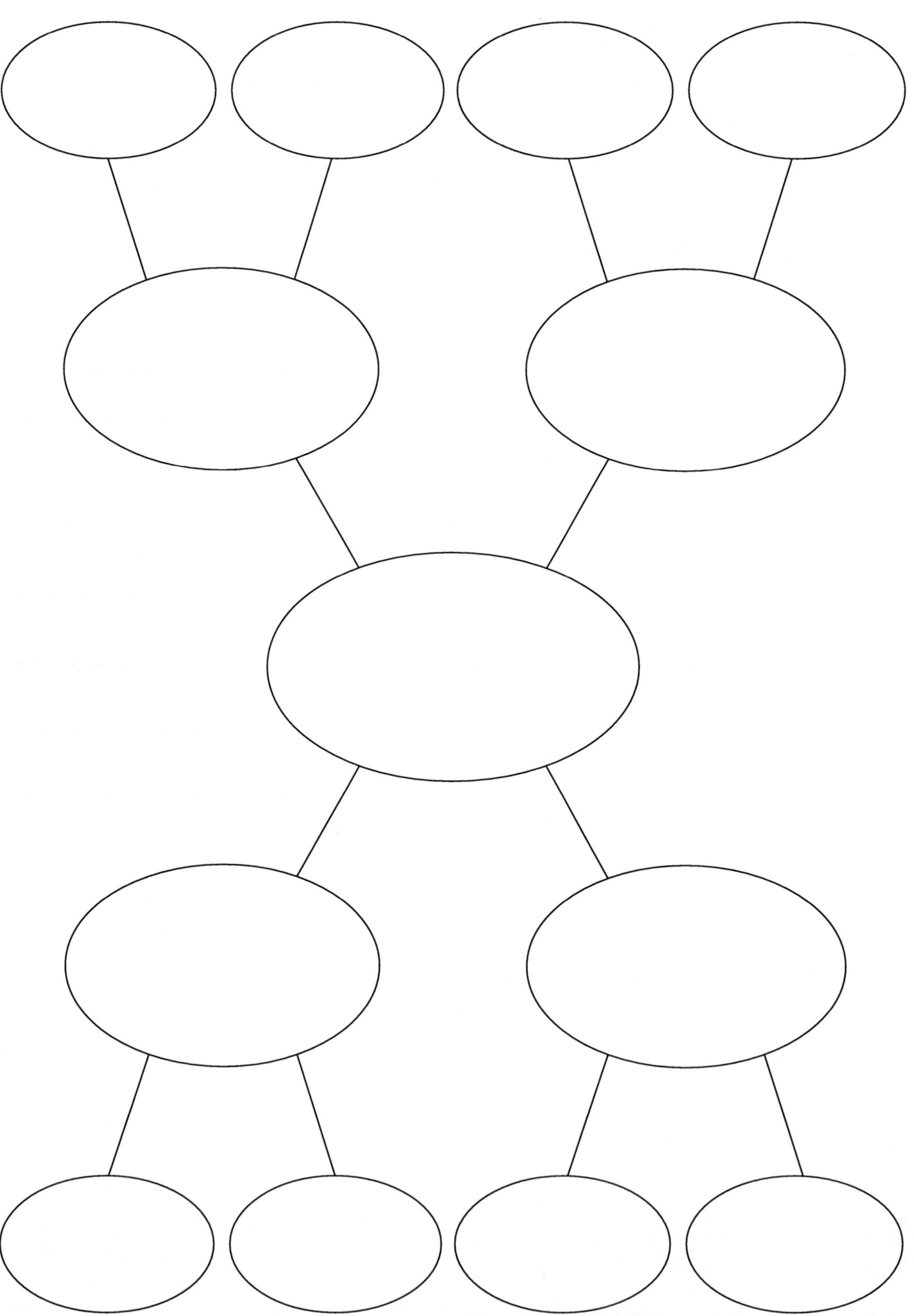

CAS: Social Studies, 7–8

Outline

I. ____

    A. ____

        1. ____

        2. ____

        3. ____

    B. ____

        1. ____

        2. ____

        3. ____

II. ____

    A. ____

    B. ____

    C. ____

Structured Notes

<table>
<tr><td>Main Ideas</td><td>Details</td></tr>
</table>

Events:

Dates:

Chronological Order Chart

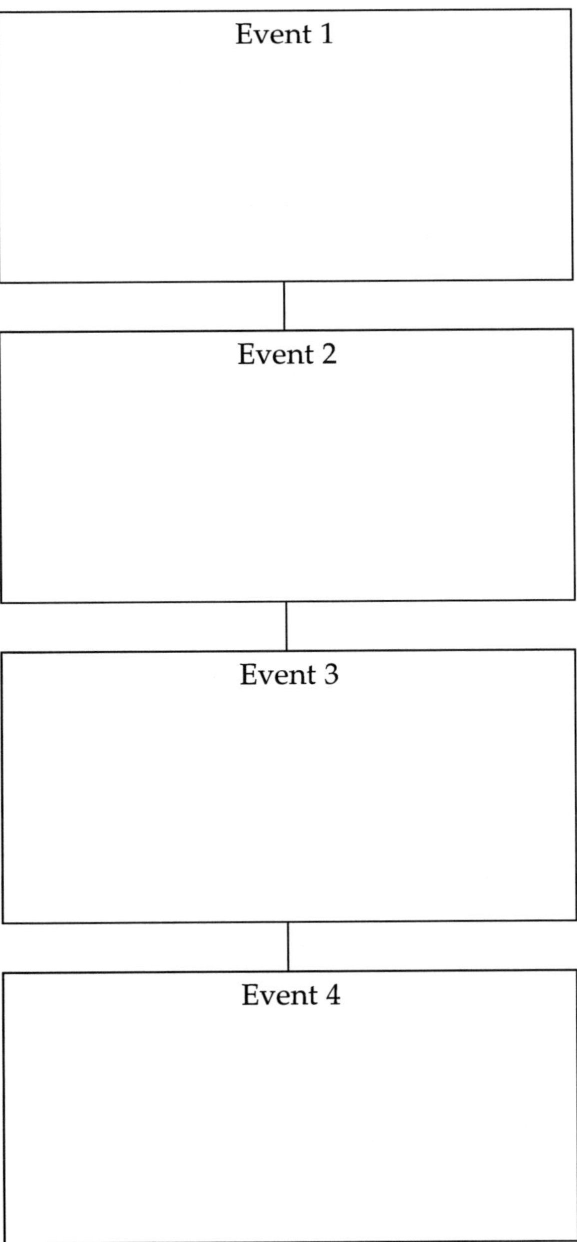

Main Idea and Details Chart

Main Idea

Detail 1

Detail 2

Detail 3

Cause-and-Effect Chart

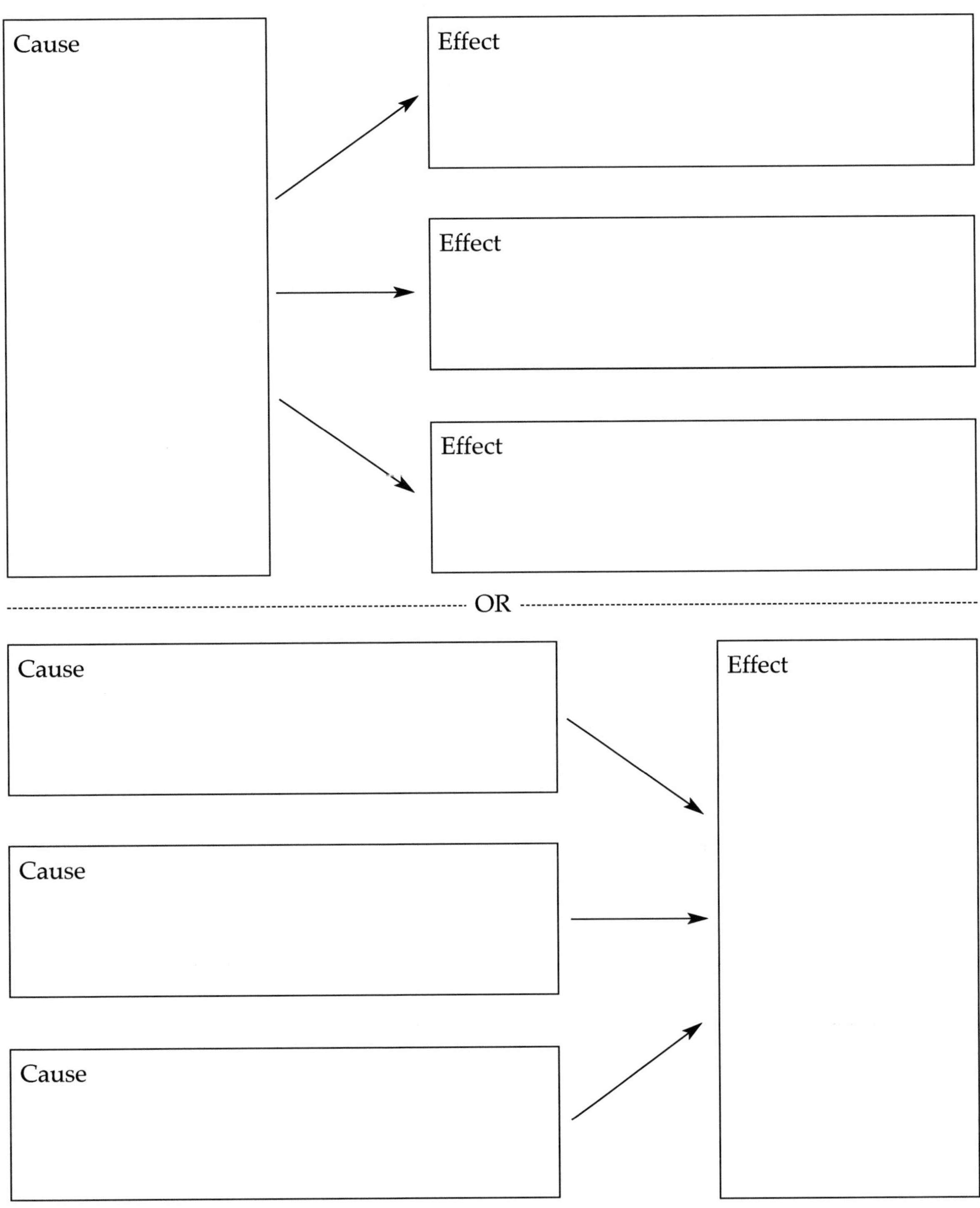

Compare-and-Contrast (Venn) Diagram

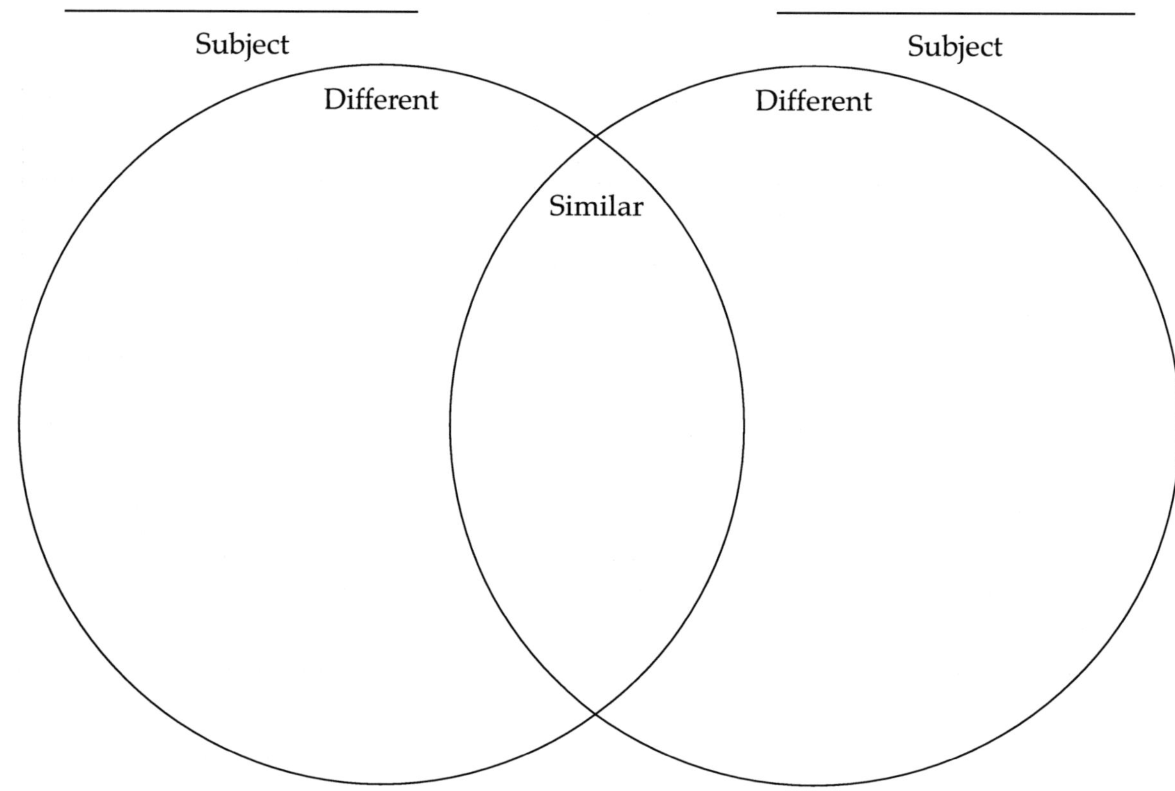

Revising Checklist

Organization	Yes	No
Did I use a logical pattern or organization?		
Did I follow my pattern consistently?		
Clarity		
Did I use signal words to clarify my pattern or organization?		
Did I make my purpose clear?		
Did I write a clear thesis statement?		
Did I include and unnecessary sentences?		
Completeness		
Did I include an introduction, a body, and a conclusion?		
Did I include enough information to support my thesis statement?		
Word Choice		
Did I use specific words rather than general words?		
Did I use vocabulary approprite for my audience?		
Other things to check for:		

Proofreading Checklist

Grammar	Yes	No
Did I write any run-on sentences?		
Did I leave any sentence fragments?		
Do my sentences all make sense?		
Do my subjects and verbs agree?		
Did I use the correct verb tenses?		
Mechanics		
Did I capitalize correctly?		
Did I use commas, periods, semicolons, and colons correctly?		
Did I use apostrophes, question marks, quotation marks, and exclamation points correctly?		
Did I spell everything correctly?		

Peer-Editing Form

Use this form to offer feedback to a classmate—and to receive feedback on your writing.

Some guidelines:

- **Start with praise.** Talk about the best, most interesting, most exiting, most insightful, or most whatever part of the piece.

- **Show respect.** As a writer yourself, you know how hard it can be to put thought on paper—you would not want your efforts to be treated lightly.

- **Stick to the point.** Address what you have been asked to address.

- **Be specific.** Saying "This section wasn't clear" is too broad and not very helpful. Something like. "Could you explain more about X? I think I'd understand better how Y happened then" gives the writer a better idea of the problem and the solution.

- **Ask questions.** Revisions are up to the writer. If you phrase your suggestions as questions ("Can you tell more about Z here?" rather than "Tell more about Z"), a writer can respond and then choose to incorporate that change or not.

Writer: ____

Title: ____

Area(s) to be discussed: ____

____

Good Points: ____

____

____

____

____

Questions: ____

____

____

____

____

Assessment Rubric for Essays

Criteria	Points				Score
	1	**2**	**3**	**4**	
Organization	Sequence of information is difficult to follow.	Some information poorly placed.	Information presented in reasonable order that reader can follow.	Information presented in logical, interesting order that reader can easily follow.	______
Content Knowledge	Insufficient grasp of information; work does not communicate adequate information.	Writer demonstrates basic understanding of concepts.	Writer is at ease with content.	Writer demonstrates full knowledge of concepts and elaborates.	______
Audience	Writer has not used appropriate tone and/or vocabulary, and has not considered audience's knowledge.	Writer has used some appropriate vocabulary, and has attempted to address audience's knowledge.	Writer has used appropriate tone and vocabulary, and has accurately assessed audience's knowledge.	Writer has used appropriate tone and vocabulary, has accurately assessed audience's knowledge, and has engaged audience with thought-provoking ideas.	______
Completeness	Not enough information; thesis statement not sufficiently supported; no or weak conclusion.	Adequate information; thesis statement supported; weak conclusion.	Sufficient information; thesis statement supported; strong conclusion.	Sufficient information; thesis statement well supported; strong conclusion.	______
Grammar and Mechanics	Piece has four or more grammatical/spelling/usage/punctuation errors.	Piece has three grammatical/spelling/usage/punctuation errors.	Piece has no more than two grammatical/spelling/usage/punctuation errors.	Piece is free of grammatical/spelling/usage/punctuation errors.	______
Other:					______

Comments

Total: ______

Answer Key

Vocabulary Strategies

Part 1: Building Vocabulary

Lesson 1: Prefixes and Suffixes

You can extend this lesson by having students find examples of words containing prefixes and suffixes in their own reading—for example, in their social studies texts. Student volunteers can write their selected words on the board, highlighting the prefixes/suffixes and explaining how they arrived at the appropriate word meanings.

Application

Answers to the second part of each question will vary. Some possible answers are given here.

1. (a); prefix *un-* ("not")
2. (c); suffixes *-ish* ("having the characteristics of") and *-ly* ("in such a manner")
3. (b); prefix *sub-* ("below")
4. (d); prefix *ex-* ("out from")
5. (b); prefix *in-* ("not") and suffix *-ible* ("able to be")

Lesson 2: Word Forms

You can extend this lesson by dividing students into teams, then writing a "core" word or a root word on the board. Teams can compete to see how many different forms of the word they can come up with. If teams are having a difficult time with this concept, you can take away the competitive aspect of the activity and simply work together using dictionaries to come up with their answers.

Application

1. (a) ; core word: tend
2. (d); core word: territory
3. (a); core word: necessary
4. (b); core word: ally (a noun)
5. (b); core word: diminish

Encourage students who need help with the definitions to use the dictionary or to work in pairs to work these meanings out.

Lesson 3: Using Context Clues

To extend the lesson, have students bring to class examples of reading material they find challenging. As a group, tackle one or two unfamiliar vocabulary words using the context clue strategies they have learned in this lesson, and any other strategies you may wish to introduce.

Application

Answers will vary, but should include the following information:

1. *dignitary:* someone of importance and high position. Examples in the text include "wealthy businessman," "important figure," and "referred to as Deacon."
2. *treatise:* a methodical written discussion or argument. Context clue is a definition found in the text: "powerful written argument."
3. *doctrine:* clearly stated principle or position in a belief system (or government policy). Context clue is a synonym: "position."
4. *caucus:* a meeting of like-minded individuals who select political candidates and establish policy. Context clue is a restatement: "This was a secret organization that met in advance of all town meetings to decide upon the slate of candidates for office and what the stands would be on various issues."

Part 2: Vocabulary in Context

Lesson 4: The Shakers and Their Villages
Activity 2

Context-clue answers are as follows. Student sentences will vary.

1.	pacifism	6.	goods
2.	conservation	7.	settlements
3.	patent	8.	monastery
4.	utopia	9.	drafted
5.	communist	10.	doctrine

Activity 3

1.	settlements	6.	drafted
2.	utopia	7.	monastery
3.	goods	8.	communist
4.	patent	9.	conservation
5.	doctrine	10.	pacifism

Lesson 5: Henry David Thoreau at Walden Pond

Activity 2

1. history
2. artifacts
3. environmental
4. society
5. slavery
6. tyranny
7. abolitionist
8. civil disobedience
9. passive resistance
10. political

Activity 3, Part I

1. abolitionist
2. tyranny
3. civil disobedience
4. environmental
5. passive resistance

Activity 3, Part II

1. history
2. slavery
3. artifacts
4. society
5. political

Lesson 6: Zora Neale Hurston and the Folklore of the Deep South

Activity 2

Context-clue answers are as follows. Student sentences will vary.

1. poverty
2. renaissance
3. rural
4. folklore
5. migration
6. anthropologists
7. stereotypes
8. plantations
9. dialect
10. prejudice

Activity 3

Zora's job:
worked as <u>anthropologist</u>
to collect <u>folklore</u>
Historical black problems:
racial <u>prejudice</u>
white <u>stereotypes</u>
struggle up from <u>poverty</u>
New York City, 1920s–1930s:
the Great <u>Migration</u>
the Harlem <u>Renaissance</u>

Folklore collected:
concerning <u>plantations</u>
in <u>rural</u> South
spoken and written in <u>dialect</u> form

Lesson 7: César Chávez and Migrant Workers in California

Activity 2

1. labor
2. migrant
3. agribusiness
4. wages
5. benefits
6. union
7. strike
8. boycott
9. activists
10. radicals

Dictionary Skills

Answers will vary. *Agribusiness* combines *agriculture* and *business*. *Brunch* combines *breakfast* and *lunch*. Other portmanteau words are *animatronics* (*animation* and *electronics*) and *smog* (*smoke* and *fog*).

Activity 3

1. labor
2. union
3. activists
4. radicals
5. strike
6. boycott
7. migrant
8. wages
9. benefits
10. agribusiness

Lesson 8: Commuters and the Suburbs

Activity 2

1. trend; "general movement"
2. affluence; "wealth"
3. middle class; "The rich," "the poor," "But the"
4. suburbs; "outside the cities"
5. commuting; "highway system," "jobs in the city"
6. baby boom; "increased the number"
7. racism; ". . . many people still . . . skin color"
8. exurbs; "the suburbs beyond the suburbs"
9. sprawl; "uncontrolled development"
10. telecommuter; "works from home"

Activity 3

Causes and Indicators: trend; affluence; middle class; baby boom; racism

Two Ways to "Go": commuting; telecommuter

Effects: suburbs; sprawl; exurbs

Mystery Phrase: Chasing the American dream

Reading Strategies

Part 1: Prereading

Lesson 1: Previewing

You may reinforce students' prereading skills by having them use their actual social studies texts. They can apply these strategies either to the chapter they are now working with or to an upcoming chapter.

Application

Answers will vary, but should include the following information:

1. The title tells us that the main topic pertains to growth of a new nation. It also tells us what time period is being covered (nineteenth century), but does not give the country's name.

2. The two subheadings reveal the two main themes: physical expansion and technological improvements (pertaining to both transportation and communication).

3. Boldfaced words are roads, canals, steamship, National Road, Erie Canal, *Clermont* (again, all pertaining to transportation and communication).

4. The first paragraph describes the doubling of U.S. territory by the early nineteenth century. The middle paragraphs describe transportation and communication issues resulting from such an immense expansion of territory and the solutions that were arrived at to address those issues. The final paragraph focuses on the dawn of steam transportation.

5. Graphic elements are the time line and the steamship drawing. The time line contains many references to inventions and technological developments. The drawing highlights one of the major new developments in transportation of that era.

Lesson 2: Predicting

Again, have students use their actual social studies texts or other current classroom materials to practice their prereading strategies in everyday context.

Application

Answers will vary, but should include the following information:

1. Readers should be able to predict that this passage is about the transportation and the communication issues facing early nineteenth-century America and what improvements and innovations resolved them.

2. This passage focuses primarily on territorial expansion (first paragraph), the need for better transportation and communication (all paragraphs), the National Road (third paragraph), canals (fourth paragraph), and steamships (last paragraph).

3. Answers will vary.

4. The main idea might be that American innovation and new technology successfully met the transportation and communication challenges of an expanding nation.

Lesson 3: Prior Knowledge

Students—especially those who lack confidence—tend to underestimate the amount of prior knowledge they really have. Encourage them to think about their own personal experiences and previous reading about a given topic as you introduce it in class. They will eventually become more confident as they realize how much they really know.

Application

All answers will vary.

Lesson 4: Purpose

Author purpose and author bias are extremely important concepts for students to understand, since many readers assume that whatever they see on a printed page or on a computer screen is inherently "true." Use a newspaper to explain the difference between an opinion piece (like an editorial), which reveals bias, and a straight news story, which is generally more balanced and objective. You and your students can find many more examples showing different kinds of author bias both in print and on the Web.

Application

1. Answers will vary.

2. Answers will vary, but should include the following: The author's purpose was most likely to teach. (NOTE: You might choose to address author bias here. The author of this passage is clearly disposed to think highly of both American territorial expansion and its innovative spirit; the tone is very upbeat.)

Part 2: Reading Strategies

Lesson 5: Introduction to Reading Strategies

To reinforce each of these reading strategies and to familiarize students with the use of graphic organizers, try applying each strategy to a chapter in your social studies text. You may choose to do this together as a whole-class activity, or you may want to assign it as homework or as a small-group project.

Lesson 6: KWL

Application

All answers will vary.

Quiz

1.	(d)	4.	(c)
2.	(b)	5.	(a)
3.	(d)		

Lesson 7: SQ3R

Application

All answers will vary.

Quiz

1.	(c)	4.	(c)
2.	(a)	5.	(a)
3.	(d)		

Lesson 8: Semantic Web

Application

All answers will vary, but semantic webs created by students should include at least some of the following:

Main idea: African Americans helped the Union win the Civil War.

Details: About 200,000 escaped slaves were paid laborers for Union during war.

Many black regiments fought heroically—like 54th Massachusetts Regiment's attack on Fort Wagner.

186,000 African-American soldiers in Union army; 29,000 in navy; 38,000 died.

Fought in at least 39 major battles and 400 smaller fights.

Other African Americans helped as spies, scouts, nurses, teachers.

Quiz

1.	(b)	4.	(d)
2.	(a)	5.	(d)
3.	(b)		

Lesson 9: Outline

Application

Answers will vary, but a completed outline might look like this:

Hawaiian Islands

I. Geography

  A. Settled well over 1,000 yrs ago

  B. Volcanic islands

    1. lava from volcanoes under ocean floor

    2. stretch over hundreds of miles

    3. no near neighbors

      (a) Aleutian Islands 2,000 miles north

      (b) Marquesas Islands 2,000 miles south

II. Settlement/Culture

  A. Founded by Polynesians from other South Pacific islands

    1. arrived over 1,000 years ago

  B. Unique Hawaiian culture developed

    1. no foreigners until Capt. Cook, 1778

Quiz

1.	(b)	4.	(d)
2.	(c)	5.	(a)
3.	(d)		

Lesson 10: Structured Notes

Application

Answers will vary.

Quiz

1. (a)
2. (a)
3. (d)
4. (c)
5. (d)

Part 3: Postreading

Lesson 11: Summarizing and Paraphrasing

Have students practice summarizing versus paraphrasing as they use their actual social studies texts. You might also select some well-known primary source documents (like the Preamble to the Constitution or the Gettysburg Address) and have students summarize and/or paraphrase them. If this is proving difficult for some learners, you can assign the activity as group work.

Application

All answers will vary.

Quiz

1. (b)
2. (c)
3. (d)
4. (b)
5. (a)

Part 4: Reading in Social Studies

Lesson 12: Common Features and Patterns in Social Studies Reading

This lesson introduces features and patterns that distinguish social studies texts from other texts. This is a good time to discuss primary versus secondary sources.

Lesson 13: Maps, Photos, and Drawings

As you introduce this lesson, be sure to point out common map features using examples from your classroom and from students' social studies texts. You can also bring in newspapers and magazines so that students can study the photos that have been selected for publication. Why were these particular images chosen? What messages are they sending/reinforcing? Is there any author/photographer bias involved?

Application

1. 12
2. Oklahoma
3. the Red and Arkansas rivers
4. at least 8
5. 1,500
6. 1,300

Lesson 14: Charts, Graphs, and Time Lines

Reinforce students' graphing skills by having them create their own graphs based on current classroom reading in their social studies texts. If this is difficult for some learners, you can assign it as a group activity.

Application

1. The dotted line shows the manufacturer's willingness to produce widgets at different prices.
2. The solid line shows the demand for widgets at different prices.
3. the equilibrium market price
4. $3
5. They are farthest apart on the far right; this shows the greatest disparity between customers' willingness to buy widgets priced at $1 and the manufacturer's desire to produce widgets priced at $5.

Lesson 15: Chronological Order

You may want to have students practice using chronological order with material from their current social studies reading using the following activity. Divide the class into small groups; then assign different sections of either the textbook chapter students are now reading or a previous chapter. Each group should list key events from their section of the reading in chronological order. They should next scramble the events on a separate sheet of paper. These scrambled lists can be photocopied, then handed out to groups for rearranging.

Application

1. (a)—4; (b)—6; (c)—2; (d)—3; (e)—5; (f)—1
2. Answers will vary, but students should see that chronological order is a logical

pattern for this sort of historical narrative to use.

3. Answers will vary, but you should help students understand that most history texts consist of straightforward historical narrative, proceeding from earlier eras to later ones. This is a logical way in which to show the evolution of cultural and political history, as well as geologic and geographic history.

4. Answers will vary.

5. Answers will vary.

6. Answers will vary, but you might remind students of the "flashback" technique, in which the story jumps back and forth between present and past.

Lesson 16: Main Idea and Details

Try quizzing students on their current social studies reading as you apply the concept of main idea versus details. Read aloud certain key statements from their social studies textbook, one by one. Students should be able to tell you whether each statement is a main idea or a detail. This can be done orally or in writing, depending on the level of formality you choose, and whether your students need the visual reinforcement of written text to facilitate their comprehension.

Application

1. (a) D   (e) D
   (b) D   (f) D
   (c) MI   (g) MI
   (d) D   (h) D

2. two

3. Topic sentence 1 is located at the very end of paragraph 1. Topic sentence 2 is located at the very beginning of paragraph 2.

4. Answers will vary, but many students may feel that it is easier to grasp the main idea when the topic sentence appears at the beginning of the paragraph.

Lesson 17: Cause and Effect

Cause and effect can often be applied to current news stories, from the results of a natural disaster to the reasons for (and fallout from) a political crisis, or the causes and results of a Wall Street panic. Using news items from the real world can help students see that the reading strategies they are learning about in class can be used every day in a meaningful context.

Application

Answers will vary.

Lesson 18: Compare and Contrast

Have students compare/contrast two world figures, two geographic regions, two political parties or ideologies, or two countries from their current social studies textbooks. These comparisons should be in written form—either informal (using a simple graphic organizer) or more formal (in carefully written paragraphs). Or, you can have students work in groups to present their information in a debate format—each group studying one side of the person, place, or issue.

Application

Answers will vary.

Writing Strategies

Part 1: Prewriting

Lesson 1: Writing Process Review

Students may be familiar with the writing process. Even if they are not, this review lesson will give students a condensed list of the steps in the writing process and prepare them for the work they will be doing in the subsequent lesson.

Lesson 2: Brainstorming

Encourage students to have fun with brainstorming; they'll have plenty of time to get serious a little later on. If they have a hard time coming up with ideas on space exploration, you might want to jog them with ideas such as these:

aliens	novas
anti-gravity	planets
Apollo 13	remote sensing
Neil Armstrong	robotics
astronauts	rockets
black holes	satellites
galaxies	science fiction
John Glenn	solar system
gravity	Space Shuttle Discovery
Hubble Telescope	space station
Mars	sun
Christa McAuliffe	sunspots
meteorology	Star Trek
missiles	Voyager
NASA	

Lesson 3: Narrowing Your Topic

Here's a tip you can give your students about narrowing the topic. You may want to have them limit the subject to one person, example, or event that illustrates or represents the topic. Or, they may want to limit their choice to a specific time frame, place, or a specific procedure or method in answer to the question they are being asked to write about. Encourage students to review their brainstorming webs to determine what they know and are interested in pertaining to the general topic. The more control a student has over the topic, the more likely it is that the finished piece will be interesting to write—and to read.

Lesson 4: Purpose

You may want to discuss some of the many purposes people have for writing, including those suggested on the student page. Students may also have other ideas; you may want them to talk about the types of writing they do regularly and their purposes for undertaking the task. It may be worthwhile to differentiate between narrative and expository writing if students are more familiar with writing fictional stories or personal anecdotes.

You may also want to discuss generating topic sentences, or thesis statements. One way to come up with a thesis statement is to think about your narrowed topic and your purpose

for writing about it, then take some kind of stance that can be elaborated on. One succinct statement that tells what the essay will show can often be used as a thesis statement.

Lesson 5: Audience

Although the audience for the written pieces created in response to this text will be the teacher and/or peers, it is important that students be aware that this is not always the case. Even when the audience is the classroom teacher, thinking about that audience's background knowledge of, interest in, and expectations about a written piece influences diction and tone.

Part 2: Writing Strategies

In this section, all student essays will vary.

Lesson 6: Drafting

This introductory lesson emphasizes the steps in drafting (there is always more than one draft!) and outlines the types of writing and organizational patterns that will be addressed in the text.

Lesson 7: Chronological Order

It might be helpful to tell students that the word *chronological* comes from the Greek word *chronos*, which means "time." Invite them to come up with some other words that start with *chron-*, such as *chronic*, *chronicle*, or *chronometer*.

At the end of the paragraph on tools of history, students are asked the question, "What do you think our new age is being called?" Encourage them to discuss what they think might be the name of the new age. You might suggest that the computer and other technologies are now being considered the tools that cultivate our lives. Many historians are calling this period the Technology Age. Ask students to think about whether or not they think this is a good title for our times.

Try It

4   Brag practices swordplay.

3   Brag becomes a squire.

7   Brag is dubbed a knight.

5   Brag follows his knight into battle.

2   Brag moves to a castle far from home.

8   Brag trains other squires how to be knights.

6   Brag holds an all-night vigil.

1   Brag becomes a page.

List of chronological/sequential words from Sir Brag's notes: first, second, from then on, when, then, finally, night before, next day, then, now

Lesson 8: Main Idea and Details

Try It

1. The main idea of "A Quiet Revolution" is that civil disobedience is a quiet form of protest that can work to change laws.

2. Topic sentence: Henry David Thoreau wrote an essay called "Civil Disobedience," which gave a name to a form of protest that would influence world events forever more.

3. Supporting details: Gandhi successfully used civil disobedience to stage a protest against laws that permitted Indians to be treated unfairly.

Dr. Martin Luther King, Jr. used civil disobedience to change laws for equality for African Americans in the United States.

Civil disobedience is not easy.

Civil disobedience can effect change for those who are patient enough to wait to see the changes happen over time.

Good Writing Tips

Transition words:

paragraph 1: But in reality

paragraph 2: At first

paragraph 3: It wasn't long . . . From then on . . .

paragraph 4: But . . . however . . .

Lesson 9: Cause and Effect

Try It

1. Effect = Rosa Parks was arrested

    Cause = she would not give up her seat

2. Effect = the Supreme Court passed a law making it illegal to segregate buses

    Cause = because the African American community staged a boycott of the buses

Good Writing Tip

Possible answers for cause-and-effect words:

. . . her actions **began** a chain of events . . .; **Then** he said . . .

You may want to point out to students that the driver's message implies the *if . . . then* cause-and-effect statement. The statement by the driver could read: *If you don't stand up, then I'll have you arrested.*

. . . driver brought charges against her and as a result; four days later . . .; Because of the chain of events . . .; . . . which resulted in . . .

Lesson 10: Compare and Contrast

Good Writing Tip

compare words: common, both, and

contrast words: differences, but, on the other hand

Try It

common, Both, In addition, further, larger, different, too, also, on the other hand, whereas

Possible Venn diagram entries:

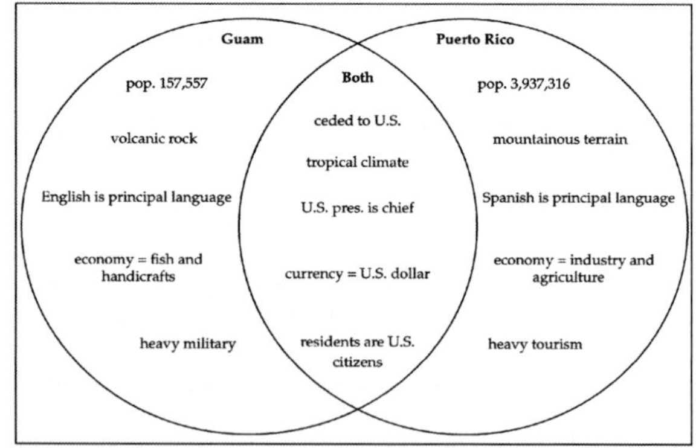

Share Your Bright Ideas

We want to hear from you!

Your name____Date____

School name____

School address____

City ____State ______Zip___________Phone number (______)_______________

Grade level(s) taught_________Subject area(s) taught____

Where did you purchase this publication?____

In what month do you purchase a majority of your supplements?____

What moneys were used to purchase this product?

____School supplemental budget ____Federal/state funding ____Personal

Please "grade" this Walch publication in the following areas:

Quality of service you received when purchasing ....A B C D

Ease of use..A B C D

Quality of content..A B C D

Page layout ....A B C D

Organization of material ....A B C D

Suitability for grade level ....A B C D

Instructional value...A B C D

COMMENTS:____

____

What specific supplemental materials would help you meet your current—or future—instructional needs?

____

Have you used other Walch publications? If so, which ones?____

May we use your comments in upcoming communications?   ____Yes   ____No

Please **FAX** this completed form to **888-991-5755**, or mail it to

Customer Service, Walch Publishing, P. O. Box 658, Portland, ME 04104-0658

We will send you a **FREE GIFT** in appreciation of your feedback. **THANK YOU!**